Prestigious Watches

Edited by
Sophie Ann Terrisse

BW Publishing, Inc.

in association with

Rizzoli International Publications, Inc.

First published in the United States of America in 1997 by

Ms. Caroline Childers and
BW Publishing, Inc.
11 West 25th Street, New York NY 10010
in association with
Rizzoli International Publications, Inc.
300 Park Avenue South, New York NY 10010

ISBN: 0-8478-1991-4

Library of Congress Catalog Card Number: 96-96942

Disclaimer: The information contained in *Prestigious Watches* has been provided
by third parties. While we believe that these sources are reliable, we assume
no responsibility or liability for the accuracy of technical details contained in this book.

Every effort has been made to locate the copyright holders of materials
used in this book. Should there be any errors or ommisions, we apologize
and shall be pleased to make acknowledgements in future editions.

Logo by Danielle Loufrani

Printed in Hong Kong

Cover photo: Minute repeater in 18K pink gold with skeletonized movement
decorated by hand from Vacheron Constantin's "Les Complications" collection.

Opposite Page: Automatic perpetual calendar chronograph in platinum
by Chopard.

Contents

Foreword

When the quartz movement was first invented in the 1970s, it seemed that the tradition of mechanical watchmaking would fade into the background. But the world underestimated the human love for fine hand-crafted objects, and the horologist's passion for his Art. In response to the competition, the artisans of true watchmaking designed new timepieces housing breathtakingly complex movements in slimmer, more elegant cases. These timepieces linked past and present, combining the elements of improved classic movement structures with new linear, modern designs.

The dedication of today's watchmakers, a close-knit family of artists and technical wizards, who still collaborate to perfect their Art and to make each instrument a masterpiece of precision and elegance, is an inspiration. Every year, like clock-work, entirely new timepieces emerge from their efforts, and improvements are made on sound classic designs.

Watches like these are works of Art, and this is what we aim to share with you. The aesthetic of the timepiece are what first kindled our interest in the subject, and we hope that you too will appreciate this journey for the eyes: the extensive selection of materials — platinum, gold, sapphire glass, precious gems and leather; the shape of a sculpted case, whether solid and thick, breath-takingly intricate, or just simple and linear; the details of a face which may display Roman numerals, a guilloché, a cabochon index or an aperture through which a bridge, a wheel, a tourbillon or the hour will appear. Take your time and observe the intricacies of the wheels, the luster of precious metals, and the fluidity of lines.

Through the contemplation of beauty, your understanding, appreciation and passion for watches can only be deepened.

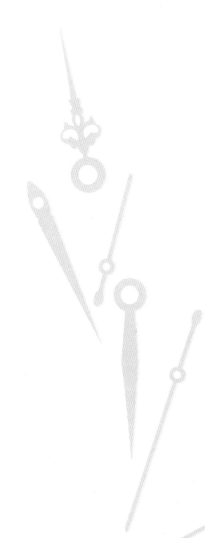

Acknowledgments

This book could not have been produced without the assistance of many people. Among those who generously shared with us their knowledge of watchmaking and their experience in the world of the Watch Industry, we want to thank Mr. Peter Laetsch, President of the Federation of the Swiss Watch Industry in the United States, and his wife, Sylvia, for their enduring friendship and support; Mr. Joe Thompson, editor-in-chief of Europa-Star, and Ms. Norma Buchanan, of National Jeweler Magazine, for their advice; and Mr. William Schmid and his wife Micheline, from the Hôtel de la Lande in Switzerland, for giving me the most delectable introduction to true watchmaking.

We are indebted to all individuals and companies that have helped find photographs and permitted us to use them. We want to express our sincere gratitude and appreciation to: Mrs. Béatrice Vuille, Mr. Rodolph Schultess, Mrs. Huguette Imhoff and Mr. Nelson Lucero from Bruguet, for their time and attention, and for allowing us to feature their sumptuous photos; Mr. and Mrs. Alain Silberstein for sharing with us their vision; Mr. Larry Geisler and Mr. Vincent Perriard from Audemars Piguet for their effective kindness, Mr. Benjamin Kaiser, Mr. Jacques-Philippe Auriol and Ms. Linda Passaro from Baume & Mercier; Mr. Destino and Ms. Anne Holbach from Cartier; Mrs. Caroline Gruosi-Scheufele and Ms. Annick Benoit Godet from Chopard; Mr. William Furhmann and Rachele from Chopard USA for their always elegant expression of trust and support; Mrs. Slider, Mr. Monti and Mr. Brandt from Eberhard; and Mr. Herman Plotnik and Ms. Michelle Dileo from Vacheron Constantin for their diligence.

We also want to thank the many people who provided a wealth of information to complete this book, including Mr. Roberto Bernasconi and Mr. Peter Bigler from Ulysse Nardin; Mr. Al Castorina, Mr. Renato Tomassini and Ms. Roberta Nass from IWC; Ms. Nancy Fox Mr. Henry-John Belmont from Jaeger-LeCoultre; Mr. Henry Hendelman, Ms. Tania Edwards and Ms. Irene Stevens from Patek Philippe; Ms. Evelyne Ménager and Mr. Daniel Bogue from Chaumet; Ms. Mary Kay Rafferty from Bvlgari; Mr. Jean Siegenthaler from Editions Scriptar SA; and Ms. Catherine Cardinal from the Musée International d'Horlogerie de La-Chaux-de-Fonds, for her invaluable research work on the history of watchmaking.

This book required the careful attention of all those involved in its production: Paul and Guy Leibstein and their eye for color. Christian Bock for the many hours of scanning and proofing. Mr. Mark Solomon who completed printing of the book. We also thank Mrs. Solveig Williams and Mr. John Brancati at Rizzoli International Publications who guided us through all phases of production. Finally, we are especially grateful to Mr. Joseph Zerbib for his unwavering support instrumental in making *Prestigious Watches*.

Caroline Childers
Publisher

Timeless Virtuosity

Peter Laetsch
President
Federation of the Swiss Watch Industry
New York

The Federation of the Swiss Watch Industry is dedicated to promoting Swiss watchmaking. The industry's worldwide reputation rests upon the discipline and craftsmanship of generations of our country's artisans. We seek to uphold their image by educating the public about the Art of Horology and the people who spend countless hours toiling over their art, creating "chefs d'oeuvres" revered by those who recognize excellence.

This book explores both watches and the watchmaking industry. It informs the reader about modern innovations and how watches have evolved from early forms into complex timekeeping devices. Today our industry is a fast-paced enterprise, and watches are created as both technological masterpieces and fashion accessories. Passed down from generation to generation, watches reflect the status, lifestyle and interest of those who appreciate, wear and collect them.

The average American consumer owns three to four timepieces, ranging from fashion watches to specialty pieces such as chronographs and complicated watches.

At either end of the spectrum, the decision-making process in choosing a timepiece is complex.

Consumers desire the romantic appeal inherent in fine bejeweled and precious metal watches. Yet part of the allure of these watches depends upon the consumer's comprehension of the technology apparent in fine timepieces. There is also the marvel of the numerous watch "complications" miniaturized and housed within a single watch. Designs of uncompromising taste are also a part of the romanticism of hand-craftsmanship, an art which has been proudly perfected throughout Switzerland's rich horological history.

It is through an understanding of these components that greater appreciation of the miracle of Switzerland's luxury timepieces is realized.

The First Pages of Time

John Brancati
Vice President
Rizzoli Bookstores, Inc.
New York

In the course of my professional career as a bookseller, I have learned to identify a number of general categories of books that always seem to sell well. The top three being most notable are books on sex, Italian food and Cats & Dogs. Their appeal must be based on the sensory satisfaction which accompanies our interaction with these indulgences.

Although not among the top three, but not very far removed, the interest in books on watches is great. Whether it is a book on a specific brand or a general survey, books on watches are in demand. As with our other indulgences, the watch carries a special significance for its owner. Most of us don't always wear a tie, or carry a purse, but we usually always wear a watch. It is a true reflection of one's spirit for only the owner gazes into its face.

The book which you hold now in your hands will be a useful reference for the collector and the beginner alike. The information and illustrations combine to make this an elegant volume which will entertain and inform. And, just as a good watch looks well on its owner, this volume will be welcome on any bookshelf.

Introduction

When we glance at the timepiece on our wrist, we never doubt the accuracy of the information provided by the two endlessly rotating hands on the dial. We take for granted when viewing our wristwatches that the results of recording the time of our life may be simply attributed to the wealth of ingenuity of a few.

We forget to give credit to the inventiveness, creativity and obsession of the founders of the Art of Time: Sung, Copernicus, Ptolemy, Galileo, Huygens, Jacquet-Droz, Breguet, Patek, Vacheron, Audemars, and all other great watchmakers, as well as their heirs, the thousands who have worked soundlessly to make the rhythmical beauty of our watches.

A glance at the more than two-thousand year history of time and chronometry clearly shows that today's watch is one of the most fascinating inventions of man's intelligence. Starting with the drafting of calendars in early cultures and continuing through the creation of simple sundials and water-clocks to the first geared clocks.

Mathematical, physical and technological explorations paired with artistic and handicraft skills, rewarded mankind not only with increasingly accurate and even more complicated clocks, but also with the progressive miniaturization culminating in the highly complicated, yet very precise and small wristwatch.

In the context of the history of time as a whole, Swiss watchmaking, with nearly 300 years of history, takes up only a very small period.

Seen rather as an accessory and, as such, something inexpensive and not worth collecting, wristwatches used to be of no great interest to clock collectors. Since the beginning of the 1980's, a remarkable change has taken place in respect of the wristwatch as a collectors item.

The discovery that a high-quality wristwatch combines technical perfection, aesthetic and practical value has led to a new environment where the search for such watches has rapidly exceeded the available supply.

In the circle of collectors and admirers of antique and new wristwatches, there are a handful of names which stand for high-quality and prestige in the watch industry.

The story behind a few of these brand names, and their wristwatch creations are the subject of this book. And while it is impossible for all names to be mentioned, these pages remain as a passport showing that their outstanding accomplishments remain timeless.

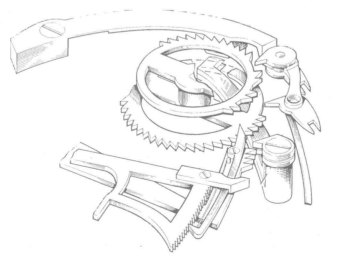

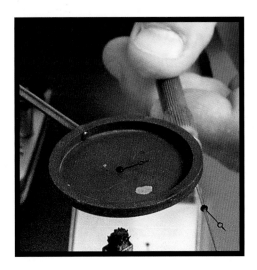

Imagine if you had to carry with you a small sundial and compass to tell the time. Or maybe someone hired you to work for as long as sand ran through the hour-glass. Perhaps you measured your birthdays by the number of full moons you had seen in your life or how many times the land beneath you was covered in snow. For many years, the birth and death of people and livestock marked the passage of time. The way people have conceived time has changed dramatically since then. And yet every civilization has in some way attempted to categorize,

Lines of Time

calculate and harness time, depending on the climate and beliefs of an area. Sundials are ineffectual in regions covered with cloudy skies. Far from the equator, the sun comes out for a few months and then disappears below the horizon for a few more. There are still cultures around the world who use different calendars. Annual holidays like the Chinese New Year and the Jewish Rosh Hashana fall on different times of the year. Who is to say that the manner in which we measure time is the correct and natural way? Animals do not measure and

yet they have an innate sense which tells them when to mate and hibernate. A revealing study was done on our own internal clocks and cycles. A man was placed in a cell below the surface of the earth, hidden from television, radio, changes in the weather or any other means to indicate the passing of time. He was supplied with provisions and books. Within a few weeks, each activity that he took on was carried out for a significantly longer period of time. He slept longer; he read longer. In short, he had adapted to a time cycle totally different than

our own. It was only one study and yet it proved in some way that time will never truly be captured by the devices of mankind. There are too many conflicting clocks and schedules. Our measurement of time today is a remarkable achievement based upon centuries of astronomical and mathematical studies. Still we have not yet developed a calendar with equal months and a consistency that will not require continual adjustments, such as leap year. There will always be room for study and growth to fuel a history of time that will continue forever.

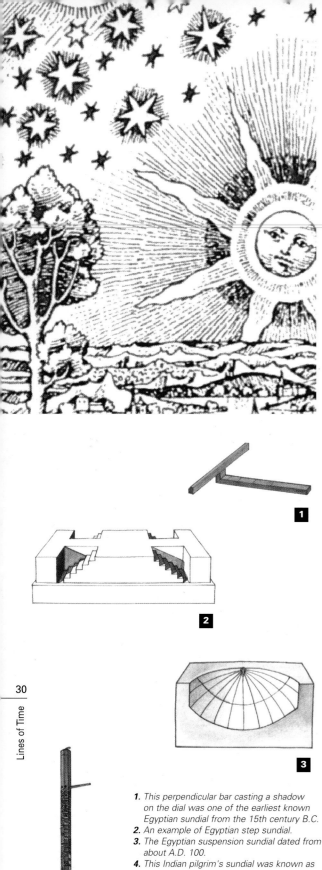

1. This perpendicular bar casting a shadow on the dial was one of the earliest known Egyptian sundial from the 15th century B.C.
2. An example of Egyptian step sundial.
3. The Egyptian suspension sundial dated from about A.D. 100.
4. This Indian pilgrim's sundial was known as the "fakir's stick." A shadow was cast by a peg shifted to one of its engraved eight scales according to the season.

PREVIOUS PAGE

Illumination illustrating "L'Horloge de Sapience"
The illuminator represented the diverse time-measuring instruments in use in the mid-fifteenth century. Brussels, Bibliotheque Royale.

THE ROLE OF RELIGION

Religion helped to create a need for time measurement. Orthodox religious practices such as prayer formed the basis for one of the earliest time measurement milestones. In the fifth century, St. Benedict dictated that prayers would take place at certain times of the day: midnight, 3 a.m., dawn, sunrise, tertia (halfway between sunrise and midday), sexta (midday), nona (mid-afternoon), vespers (one hour before sunset), and compline (9 p.m.). These were known as the "canonical hours," a crucial element in the monk's search for salvation.

EARLY INSTRUMENTS

During daylight hours, increments of time were marked by the sundial. Of all instruments used to keep track of time, the sundial has perhaps been the most consistently used. The earliest records of this device were found in the Book of Isaiah, where a passage describes a sundial which dated back to about 700 B.C. However, it is likely that they were used much earlier than this date. Their complexity ranged from a post in the ground with markers around it to a flat, calibrated dial with a pointer affixed at a 90-degree angle. There were also public versions with an obelisk placed at the center of a plaza. In each case, the sundial worked using the shadow of the sun to show local apparent solar time. Though sundials provide accurate measurements during the day, they are useless after sundown. For night-time prayer, monks were required to stay up to wake others at the appropriate times.

The earliest records of an automated timekeeping device was recorded by a monk named Jocelyn de Brakelond, who wrote about a fire which took place at Bury St. Edmunds in Suffolk, England on the night of June 23, 1198. The church, which was reputed to house the body of a saint was one of England's primary pilgrimage centers. Because of its financial and spiritual significance, the people tried to save the church at all costs. "All of us ran together and found the flames raging beyond belief and embracing the whole refectory and reaching up nearly to the beams of the church," de Brakelond wrote. "So the young men among us ran to get water, some to the well and others to the clock." It might seem curious as to why they ran to the church clock to extinguish the fire. Yet it makes sense when you understand that these early clocks were powered by water. Water clocks were widely used throughout England and northern Europe, where cloudy skies made sundials useless.

Earlier versions of these clocks, based on a device called the clepsydra, had been used in China hundreds of years earlier.

CLEPSYDRA and WATER WHEELS

The clepsydra, or water stealer, was a tool created by the Greeks. To measure time, they marked the regulated flow of water through a small opening, such as a bucket with a tiny hole pierced in the bottom. Farmlands from this time were given an allotted supply of water to measure services. When the bucket ran dry, the farmer would pay for that "bucketful" of time.

Because recorded examples of the various clepsydra are rare, early water clocks are often missing from horological timelines. There are some examples. Buddhist monk and mathematician I-Hsing developed an astronomical clockwork instrument in 723 A.D. that he called the "Water-Driven Spherical Bird's-Eye-View Map of the Heavens." In addition, animal-powered mills known as "dry-water mills" appeared in China as early as 175 A.D. They had as their precursors hydraulic mills. The Chinese are also credited for creating what is believed to be the first water-based clock, though there is speculation that examples

also existed in Islam. One Islamic clock was driven by the weight of a large float, perhaps a block of wood, contained in a tank from which water would drain at a controlled speed. As the float descended with the falling water level, its weight operated the clock mechanism.

The most famous water clock, however, was made in China. In 1090, in the capital of the Northern Sung dynasty, a government official named Su Sung constructed a 40-foot clock which he called the "Cosmic Engine." He built the clock using a wooden model and later cast the working parts in bronze. The towering structure had a complex interior mechanism described by contemporaries as "the soul of the time keeping machine." The mechanism and its "hooks, pins, interlocking rods, coupling devices, and locks checking mutually," is believed to be the world's first escapement. This is a mechanism used in modern clocks, consisting of a rotating, notched wheel and an anchor, which alternately engages and disengages to control the movement of the wheel.

Sung's clock was powered by water held in a reservoir which was refilled periodically by a manually operated noria. The noria resembled a ferris wheel and consisted of a wheel with buckets attached to its rim. The water from the

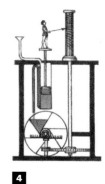
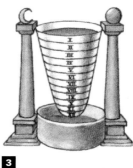

1. One of the earliest and most refined design of Egyptian water-clock dating from the 14th century B.C.
2. The solarium was the perfected Roman version of the sundial.
3. The klepsydra, ancient water-clock, was also a very sought-after decorative item.
4. A drawing of the spectacular Ktesibios' water-clock dating from the 2nd century B.C. A little statue was shifted by a float mechanism where a water-wheel turned the column with the time scale. A special device bounced a stone into a little dish and thus sounded the hours.
5. Temples and pyramids were also frequently used as sundial indicators to measure time.

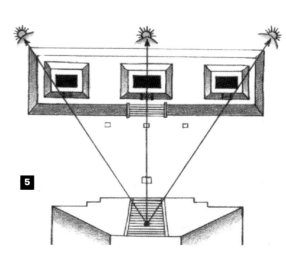

1   **2**

1. The eighteenth-century oil-clock which told time by wastage was a modern example of the earliest oil-clock used by the Romans.

2. In the third century BC, the Alexandrian mechanic Ctesibius built this water-clock. On the right, the statue of a man or cupid weeping; on the left, another figure holding a stylus which marked the hours on the column. The water which fell as tears was collected in the chamber placed under the first statue and flowed slowly into another chamber. Here a float rose gradually with the level of the water and raised the cogged rod, which imparted a circular motion to a toothed wheel. Hinged to it was a hand showing the hours as it moved. In Ctesibius's clepsydra, the float probably raised the second statue so that the stylus could gradually trace the various subdivisions of the day which (as may be seen from the nineteenth century reproduction) were of different lengths according to the month of the year.

3. One of the Ancient world's biggest water-clock resided on the "Tower of the Winds" in Athens.

3

reservoir was siphoned to a constant level water tank, where it was scooped up by a large waterwheel which turned the clock. The waterwheel turned a series of shafts, gears, and wheels, which in turn worked the bells and drums that announced the time.

Simultaneously, the escapement kept the movement at an even pace by a complex arrangement of balances, counterweights, and locks. Together these mechanisms divided the flow of water into equal parts by repeated weighing, automatically dividing the revolution of the wheel into equal intervals.

Another element of Sung's water clock was its celestial globe, a spherical model showing the positions of the stars and other celestial bodies. The clock also contained an armillary sphere, another astrological model consisting of several solid rings, all circles of a single sphere, used to display relationships among the principal planets. A chain continually and slowly turned the armillary sphere and globe.

The clock's 40-foot tower was destroyed by the Chin Tartars, who captured Kaifeng in 1126 and brought the clock to Peking. Sung's creation has only recently been recognized as a precursor to modern clockmaking. Other mishaps threatened the clock's place in history.

In 1195 the armillary sphere was struck by lightening but later repaired. Then, the precious celestial globe was melted down for scrap and ruined. By the time the Mongols took Peking as their own capital in 1264, the clock itself wasn't working. Ultimately, even Sung's magnificent escapement was lost, and Chinese clockmakers returned to using the clepsydra. In the 14th century, the remains of Su Sung's mechanism were completely destroyed when the Ming dynasty captured Peking. A contemporary sadly reported, "Now it is said that the design is no longer known, even to the descendants of Su Sing himself." So in the 17th century, when Jesuit missionaries brought a European mechanical clock to China, the device was hailed by the Chinese as "a new European invention of dazzling ingenuity." Sung's work had been forgotten.

While the early water-clocks created by I-Hsing and Su Sung overcame the challenge of darkness faced by the sundial, they also had a basic flaw: they froze in cold weather. The sand hourglass remedied that problem but was subject to harden with moisture absorption until the glass maker's art evolved and glass could be made watertight. Even candle-clocks, which seemed a promising solution, were confined to use by the wealthy due to their need for constant upkeep.

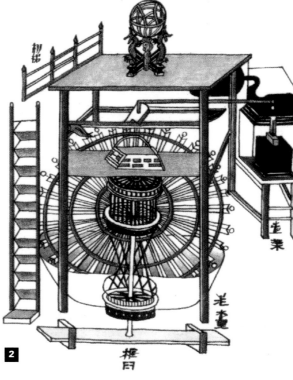

1. Earliest time telling in China consisted of a dedicated priest who regulated the village life through the indications of the different time to work, eat and pray.

2. This highly-complicated Chinese water-clock dating from the 11th century A.D. was the ancestor of Sung's first escapement clock.

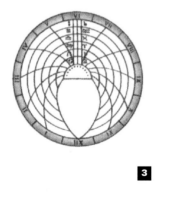

1. The sand-glass in the Middle Ages still used a principle known in antiquity.

2 & 3. The analemmata and anaforica served to divide the day into 12 equal parts throughout the year.

Despite their faults, however, the water-clocks evolved into a system of time measurement which became widely used throughout Europe. A 1268 slate was found by the Abbey of Villers outside Brussels, Belgium, which commanded: "You shall pour water from the little pot that is there, into the reservoir until it reaches the prescribed level, and you must do the same when you set the clock after compline, the final evening service, so that you may sleep soundly." Similarly, a Rule for Cistercian monks stated that the "sacrist roused by the sound of the clock shall ring the church bell."

Eventually, societal shifts necessitated a more precise method of timekeeping. None of these early clocks had a face. Specific hour markers were unnecessary, as the emphasis was not on marking the time of day, but rather on marking the passage of an interval or block of time. While today's view of time is based upon equally spaced intervals, such as hours and minutes, early conceptions were not so static. The length of these intervals changed according to the season. Such variations meant that the space between the hours marked in canonical law and other orthodox religious practices would lengthen and shorten, making it difficult to calibrate clock faces to the changing hour.

Astronomers and astrologers were also calling for more accurate instruments to aid them in tracking the stars and planets. Many of their ideas spilled over into the realm of time measurement. Many scientists viewed planetary systems as "giant piece[s] of celestial clockwork and God himself as the heavenly clock maker." This meant that if someone could build a clock or any other instrument to reproduce the motions of the sun and the planets, then one could capture the essence of godly things. In a sense, creating a clock meant recreating "what happened in the sky, to bring God's clockwork down to earth."

One of the most prescient thinkers was the Greek astronomer and mathematician Claudius Ptolemy. In the second century, he created the Ptolemic system, a method of calculating the movements of planets based on the assumption that they, along with the sun and stars, rotated around the earth. These mathematical circles could be visualized as great wheels revolving one around another, and were described in a famous series of Iranian poems written in 1100 by Khayyam. In his poetic phrases, he makes frequent references to the "wheel of the heavens," conjuring images of models in a darkened room with "the sun the candle" and "images revolving on the walls."

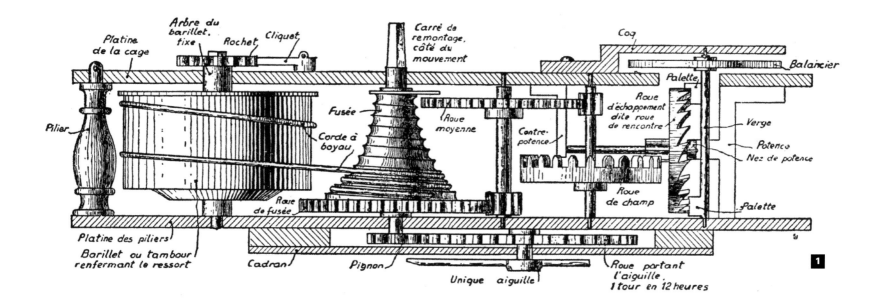

Platine de la cage
Arbre du barillet. fixe
Rochet
Cliquet
Carré de remontage, côté du mouvement
Coq
Balancier
Pilier
Fusée
Roue moyenne
Palette
Roue d'échappement dite roue de rencontre
Verge
Corde à boyau
Contre-potence
Potence
Nez de potence
Roue de champ
Platine des piliers
Barillet ou tambour renfermant le ressort
Roue de fusée
Cadran
Pignon
Unique aiguille
Palette
Roue portant l'aiguille. 1 tour en 12 heures

1

The "planet-central" system which he presented in thirteen volumes of his masterpiece Almagest were eventually replaced by Copernicus' heliocentric model. Until then, Ptolemy's theories dominated astronomical circles until the 16th century.

RISE OF THE MECHANICAL CLOCK

Ptolemy's theories had also been studied in India and Islam. In India, al-Muradi wrote extensively about elaborate gear trains with mechanisms based upon the Ptolemic system. In Islam, the astrolabe was used to calculate the positions of the planets using Ptolemy's proofs and theorems. It determined the altitude of the sun and other celestial bodies.

Scientists searched for a more accurate means of measurement and timekeeping. In the process, the old variable hour was replaced by a fixed uniform hour. However, the change would not come easily. In 1271, an Englishman teaching at Montpelier described the obstacle: "Clockmakers are trying to make a wheel which will make one complete revolution for every one of the equinoctial cycle, the day, but they cannot quite perfect their work... the method for making such a clock would be to make a disc of uniform weight... then a lead weight should be hung from the axis of that wheel and this weight would move

2

1. *Primitive watch movement. The foliot was protected by a cock equipped with one foot. The fusée was made with a a gut cord. The dial had only one hand, indicating the hours.*

2. *Rough sketch of an astrolabe used to regulate the time based on the position of the stars.*

that wheel so that it would complete one revolution from sunrise to sunset..." As his words attest, it was easy enough to spin shafts and dials with lead weights and cords, but the real test for clockmakers came in regulating the speed of that spin.

VERGE and FOLIOT SYSTEM

The solution would come with the invention of the verge and foliot system, which worked by holding back the speed at which the main shaft turned as the weight wound about it fell. There were several essential parts to the system: a crown wheel with triangular teeth; the verge or rod, which contained two projects or pallets, and was sited perpendicular to the crown so it would engage with the crown at its top and bottom; and the foliot, a crossbar balanced at the top of the verge, with weights on each end. As the crown wheel turned, one of its teeth caught the upper pallet of the verge, which held it, then released it, giving a swing to the foliot with its weights. This caused the other pallet to engage the wheel, swinging the foliot in the opposite direction. Thus, the wheel would turn one click at a time, alternately arrested by the verge's two pallets as the foliot swung back and forth.

To regulate the clock, the speed of the mechanism could be increased or decreased by moving the weights on the arms of the foliot.

The introduction of the verge and foliot has been hailed as "one of the main foundations for the development of machine technology in subsequent centuries" and "perhaps the single greatest human invention since the wheel." The earliest timepieces to utilize this system were huge iron-framed clocks created by blacksmiths to be installed in church towers. As with water-clocks, these early mechanical clocks lacked faces and hands. They were also unable to strike the hours, but instead sounded an alarm which would alert the ringer to pull the bell rope. These early clocks were probably intended to tell the time of day to the priests rather than to the community at large.

There is some controversy over the date at which the first mechanical clock was introduced. Some scholars place its invention as early as 1280. The dissension stems from the fact that most documentation offers little in the way of knowing whether or not a "clock" that has been referenced is mechanical or not. One source mentions a clock in Westminster in 1288, another in Canterbury cathedral in 1292, and

1. *This pocket-sized silver sundial was an eighteenth-century French aid to travelers. Incredibly, the dial was both portable and universal. The small octagonal plate was engraved with concentric hour scales for different latitudes and had a compass inset. The central stylus folded down for compactness and was adjustable according to latitude.*

2. *Square-shaped clock with horizontal dial. The case, made of gilded brass has openings on two sides to allow the sound of the alarm to pass. The silver dial displays Roman numerals from I to XII, repeated inside with Arabic figures from 13 to 24. The central disc is for the alarm-setting.*

OPPOSITE PAGE

Early watch with a cylinder shape made of brass and iron. The case is in gilt brass, engraved and chased with open work. The back has a medallion pierced and decorated with arabesques and flowers. This type of case resembles a small flattened drum and is characteristic of the mid 16th century German production. Both its movement and dial reflect the workmanship of german horologists of this period.

another in Paris in 1300. A clock constructed by Richard of Wallingford in about 1320 was described as a "powered astronomical model" and an "artificial universe." There is also a 1321 reference to a machine, probably a clock, which played hymns on bells in an abbey near Rouen, France. In the same year, Italian poet Dante Alighieri mentioned a clock in his Divine Comedy in a way which suggested that his readers would have been familiar with the mechanism.

However, the first clear mention of a mechanical clock comes in 1335 in reference to a timepiece in the Visconti Palace in Milan, Italy: "A heavy hammer strikes 24 hours… distinguished hour from hour, which is of great necessity to all conditions of men." A contemporary wrote: "There is a wonderful clock with a very large clapper which strikes a bell twenty-four times according to the twenty four hours of the day and night, and thus at the first hour of the night gives one sound, at the second two strokes… and so distinguishes one hour from another which is of the greatest use to men of every degree."

EARLIEST MECHANICAL WATCH and CLOCK

The earliest known builders of mechanical clocks are Jacopo di Dondi and his son Giovanni. In 1344 Jacopo created a clock for the entrance tower of the Carrara palace at Padua, which showed the phases of the moon and other astronomical features and automatically indicated "the intervals of four-and-twenty hours by day and night." This indicator is considered to be the precursor to our modern clock dial.

His son Giovanni was a lecturer of astronomy at Padua University, of medicine in Florence, and a personal physician to the Emperor Charles IV. He built what has been described as a "true mechanical clock" for the wealthy Duke Visconti of Pavia. Installed in the castle library in 1364, the clock consisted of 297 parts held together by 305 pins or wedges. It recorded minutes and hours on a small dial, measured the rising and setting of the sun, and displayed the length of the day, the days of the month, the trajectories of five planets, a perpetual calendar, an annual calendar, and even holy days and church feasts! The brass weighted balance, di Dondi's equivalent of the verge and foliot escapement, swung back and forth 43,000 times each day, giving the clock a two-second beat.

Copies of the clock's detailed blueprints can be seen in the Smithsonian Institution in Washington D.C. and in the London Science Museum.

Once the verge-and-foliot escapement became known, blacksmiths in cities throughout Europe began turning out clocks. As the clocks spread, so did the realization of their economic value.

One of the most significant things about medieval clockwork is simply that they were the very first machines made entirely of metal. Previous clocks were primarily made of wood. Clockmakers were at first largely drawn from blacksmiths, gunsmiths and locksmiths. Most were itinerant craftsmen as the large municipal public clocks and monastic clocks had to be built on site. Only later, when timepieces became smaller, could they be built in a workshop and then delivered to the user, completed and working.

New water-powered bellows were operating in blast furnaces, and waterwheels were powering mills to crush the ore to feed them. Metal-working skills spread, concentrating in areas closest to the mines themselves. The amount of metal in circulation increased considerably, as did he demand for it, particularly for the use of making clocks.

The demand for synchronized time increased the need for metal. In Paris in 1370, Charles V ordered every bell in the city to be synchronized with the sound of his clock in the tower of the Palais-Royal, so that every resident would know the king's time as it rang on the hour and quarter hour. By the end of that year, at least thirty clocks had been installed throughout Paris.

Though the number of clocks was increasing dramatically, their timekeeping abilities remained only moderately successful. A public clock built in Strasbourg, France in 1354 included a moving calendar, an astrolabe indicating the movements of the sun, moon, and planets, a statue of the Virgin Mary, and a large rooster that opened its beak, crowed, and flapped its wings. The clock itself seemed almost an afterthought, leaving one to wonder if the attention given by clockmakers to creating such ornate details may have distracted them from their commitment to precision.

On the other hand, the flourishes served a political function as well as an aesthetic one. The city clock became a source of pride, wrote Jacques Le Goff, a "marvel, an ornament, a plaything... a part of the municipal adornment, more a prestige item than a utilitarian device." Clocks indicated the time for opening and closing

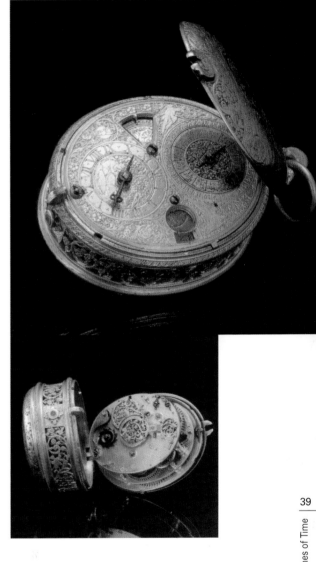

ABOVE

An oval-shaped astronomical watch made of silver and brass. Movement signed Marc Girard à Blois, France, beginning of the 17th century. Mr Girard's watch belongs to this relatively numerous series of oval watches which were fashionable as from the last quarter of the 16th century until 1630.

the gates to the city; for beginning curfew (which was when fires were extinguished, an important public safety issue for towns made primarily of wood); for watchman's hours; and for the hours of starting and stopping work. Soon cities became regimented into a fairly uniform time frame.

This system of equal hours meant that people could begin monitoring what had been previously unmeasured. In the textile towns of Flanders, where the clocks struck the working hours of the fabric workers, the "communal clock became an instrument of economic, social, and political domination wielded by the merchants who ran the commune."

However, this uniformity was local rather than national. Each city set its own zero hour, in some cases noon or midnight, but more often than not, sunrise or sunset, creating a confusion that often baffled travelers. England and most of Europe settled on a 12-hour repetition, though Italy used the 24-hour system until the 19th century. One of the most complicated systems was adopted by Nuremberg, where clocks were constructed to tell the time from sunrise to sunset, with built-in mechanisms to handle the varying length of the days throughout the year.

The mechanical clock, which had been invented to serve the needs of astrological sciences, was rapidly acquiring its own importance outside this field. Once people could time their activities, they worked and lived by the hour, creating a rhythm that continues to this day.

TABLE TOP CLOCKS

The origins of the modern wristwatch are closely tied to the development of the clock. Sigmund von Radecki wrote, "We have, over history, become slaves to measured time and so must be held by our chains... the wristwatch is the handcuff of our time." Clocks made people aware of time, which soon created a demand for more clocks. As clock-making techniques improved, it became possible to build clocks small enough to be used in private houses.

The first table clocks appeared just before 1400 and quickly became expensive status symbols. In contrast to the big tower clocks made by blacksmiths, the smaller versions created by goldsmiths and silversmiths, had faces, hour hands, and eventually minute hands. When clocks became small enough to keep on a tabletop, the next step was a portable clock, which could be worn on the body.

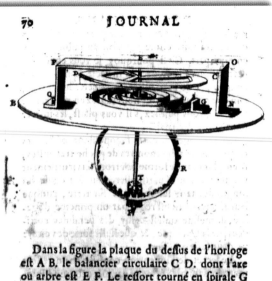

Dans la figure la plaque du deſſus de l'horloge
eſt A B. le balancier circulaire C D. dont l'axe
ou arbre eſt E F. Le reſſort tourné en ſpirale G
H M, attaché à l'arbre du balancier en M, & à la
piece qui tient à la plaque de l'horloge, en G tou-
tes les ſpires du reſſort ſe tenant en l'air ſans tou-
cher à rien. N O P Q eſt le cocq dans lequel
tourne l'un des pivots du balancier. R S eſt une
des roües dentées de l'horloge, ayant un mouvement de balancement que luy donne la roüe de
rencontre. Et cette roüe R S engraine dans le pignon T, qui tient à l'arbre du balancier, duquel
par ce moyen le mouvement eſt entretenu au-
tant qu'il eſt neceſſaire.

1

2

1. A letter by Christiaan Huygens addressed in 1675 to the "Journal des Sçavans," about the regulating spiral spring, accompanied with a drawing.

2. With a few attachments, a pendant watch could be turned into a wristwatch. This model created in the early 1910s, was indicative of the transition time from the pocket watch to the wristwatch.

THE INVENTION of THE SPRING

In Nuremberg, a metal craftsman, perhaps a locksmith, realized that a tiny metal spring could be used to replace the large weight drive used in clockmaking. However, each new invention comes with its own set of problems, and the spring was no exception. As a driving force, the spring was useless, since as it began to unwind, the clock would go fast, and as it weakened the clock would go slower and slower. To overcome this problem, an ingenious method was devised to store up energy at the beginning, progressively releasing it as the spring unwound. The solution came with the incorporation of a conical spool, or fusee, a name taken from the Latin word for a spindle.

One record mentions that the Italian architect Filippo Brunelleschi used a coiled spring drive in a clock as early as 1410. By the middle of the fifteenth century, the fusee was used in clocks collected by the very wealthy. Portraits are the primary record of these small clocks, as members of the royalty often chose to be portrayed with a table clock or timepiece affixed to the wall. A 1450 painting of a Burgundian gentleman, Jean Le-Fèvre, lord of Saint-Rémy, shows in the background a small clock shaped like a square turret, hanging from the wall by a chain.

Through its open chassis, a chime is visible on the top, and at the base, the driving gears of both the chime and movement mechanisms, composed of a spring hidden behind the molding of the base and a fusee linked to it by a rope.

The same assembly can be used to describe the wall clock that belonged to Philip the Good, Duke of Burgundy. The clock, whose movement and style was created around 1430, is now housed in the German National Museum. An inventory of the Duke's possessions, recorded in 1420, mentions a similar clock: "Item: a small square clock, gilt on the outside, and its white enameled zodiac has one bell on top to ring on the hour." Similarly, the inventory of Margaret of Burgundy three years later described "a small gilt clock… There are two panels on either side made of gilt silver, as is also the dial."

By the second half of the fifteen century, all of the components necessary for watchmaking existed. All that was needed was the reduction of their dimensions to create horology in the miniature.

DEFINING A WRISTWATCH

At this point, it is helpful to define what is meant by the words "watch" and "wristwatch." In its simplest definition, a wristwatch is a small clock worn on the wrist, a combination of bracelet and clock. The German word armbanduhr, or arm-band clock, describes the type of attachment, which can range from a heavy ring to a light chain. In terms of function, however, these watch-bracelets cannot be regarded fully as wristwatches as a wristwatch is characterized not only by its position on the arm, but also by the way by which it is used to read the time. Only the wristwatch makes it possible to read the time at a glance without any other motion.

The earliest watches needed an extra motion because the axis of their dials, from the 6 to the 12, was not parallel to the band but perpendicular to it, parallel to the arm. "Whoever wants to read time must make a movement resembling a Fascist salute," said Alfred Helwig in 1930. Moreover, women's watches had small dials and tiny hands, which made them barely visible at arm's length. The earliest watches were not true wrist-watches but decorative timepieces worn on bracelets. This new type of watch was called a bracelet-montre as jewelers and watchmakers could not agree on its exact genre. Arm-band watches, with the clock-face position familiar to us did not begin to appear until around 1850.

Before that time, watches emphasized decoration over function and reflected a high social status. Throughout the sixteenth century and into the seventeenth century watches were owned by kings, princes, and the grand bourgeois. These timepieces were wound with a key twice a day, worn around the neck or in purses or pockets, and considered accessories to elegant attire.

A letter from Jocopo Trotti, ambassador of the Este family to the court of Milan, written on July 19, 1488 to the duke of Ferrara, emphasizes this notion. "I want Your Lordship to know that M. Lodovico is secretly having three silk suits richly enhanced by very pretty pearls. All are of the same cut and are ornamented with a watch with little bells, except the one of M. Lodovico, who does not want his to strike, for he wants to be the cause of the others' ringing. And to each festive suit are affixed two short lines of verse, which you will find herewith on this little sheet.."

From the year 1500 onward, the use of watches spread throughout the courts of Europe, with the demand stimulating the rise of small-work horology. The German regions of Augsburg and Nuremberg became two of the first centers of watchmaking.

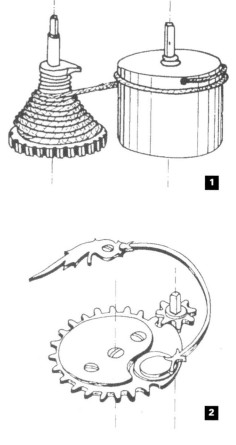

1. *Regulation of the motive power of the spring by a fusée. The fusée, shaped like a truncated cone and grooved all around in a continuous spiral from bottom to top, was originally made of a gut cord.*

2. *Regulation of the motive power of the spring by a stackfreed. Used by German horologists, the stackfreed looked like a snail-shaped cam mounted on a wheel meshing with a pinion geared on the barrel arbor.*

3. *The only escapement used in the 16th and 17th centuries was the verge escapement, or "crown wheel," was characterized by an escape wheel, dented like a crown.*

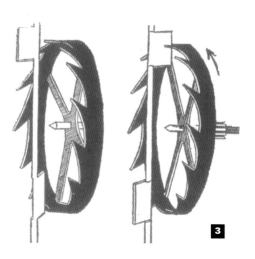

1. Watch shaped like a dog with a movement signed by Jacques Joly. Geneva, Mid-seventeenth century.

2. Rabbit-shaped watch. Movement signed Pierre Duhamel. Geneva, third quarter of the seventeenth century.

3. Table clock with automaton shaped like a dog made of wood. The animal's chest carries a large gilded brass plate with a silver dial. Connected to the balance of the movement, the glass eyes of the dog constantly move, and its jaws open and shut at each strike. At the end of its tail is a button which puts the striking back into phases.

One of the first watchmakers was Peter Henlein, a locksmith in Nuremberg. His talent is praised in an edition of the Cosmographia Pomponii Melae, published in 1512: "Every day, they invent more subtle things: It is so with Peter Henlein, still almost a child, who does work that even the most learned among mathematicians admire, for with a little iron, he produces clocks made up of many wheels that, in any position and without any weight, show and strike forty hours even when worn on the breast or in the pocket."

By 1525, other centers had sprung up in Paris, Dijon and Blois, and by the end of the Thirty Year War in 1648, German watchmaking supremacy would be eclipsed. Many Huguenots, fleeing Germany, settled in Geneva, helping to found the famous Swiss watchmaking industry. Other watchmakers settled in London. In France the industry reached such great proportions that a guild was established in 1544 by seven master watchmakers: Fleurent Valleran, Jehan de Presles, Jehan Pantin, Michel Potier, Antoine Beauvais, Nicolas Morel, and Nicolas le Contançois. In 1539 de Presles had been chosen to maintain the palace clock, a position he kept for nearly 20 years. In 1546 he was appointed the king's personal horologist.

In each region, watchmakers made timepieces which were adorned to be worn as jewelry. The focus was on beauty over function, and the watches were for the most part, inaccurate. Clients of this period favored mechanical curiosities, cherished for their complications or for the intricacy of their execution. Goldsmiths, lapidaries, jewelers, engravers and enamelers created cases of every shape and description, including ring watches, sphere- or drum-shaped watches, oval and octagonal watches, and even watches mounted on sword hilts.

The prince of Urbino received a ring crowned with a watch movement set in a gemstone. The timepiece was described as "a ring to put on the finger near the thumb, on which there was a precious stone that had a complete clock that, in addition to the line that distinguished the hours, struck for the one who wore it, at hourly intervals."

Other watches were set in perfect spheres, though it is not certain when these types of watches were introduced. One source speculates that in 1500 the German watchmaker Peter Henlein put a timekeeping mechanism inside an iron musk-ball, creating one of the first spherical watches.

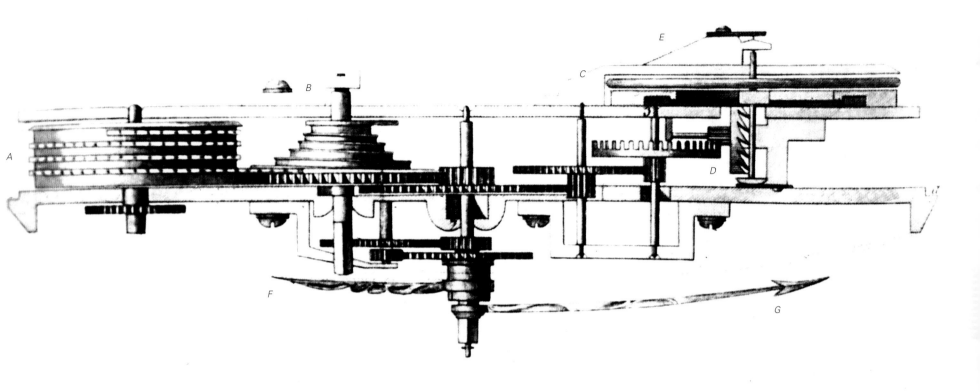

Watch movement with two plates and verge escapement.
A: barrel with chain; B: fusee; C: balance wheel; D: crown
wheel; E: cock; F: hour hand; G: minute hand.

However, the rounded shape is also said to have been borrowed from the civets or "musk apples" used in Venice and the East." Civets were small chased metal spheres, pierced with tiny holes to release the scent of perfume within.

Another popular watch shape was the drum, which evolved from the small cylindrical table clock. At first, the dial was unprotected like a table clock. It was later covered with a full lid and then pierced over each numeral to let the user read the hour. Plates on the top and bottom enclosed the cylindrical body of the case, with molded ridges slightly overlapping the circumference of the watch. Most opened on a hinge fixed at the numeral XII.

Oval or octagonal watches became popular in the last quarter of the sixteenth century, remaining in vogue until early into the next. The cases of these watches were generally made of silver or brass, or a decorative combination of the two metals. Engravers gave these watches a style characterized by mannerism, delicacy and richness of decoration. Whether created in France, Switzerland, or Germany, their decorations were copied or inspired by similar etchings, such as those by ornamentists Etienne Delaune, Antoine Jacquard, or Michel Le

Blon. Delaune's designs, for example, often featured mythological scenes or allegorical figures with florid titles like "Narcissus Falling in Love With Himself" or "Orpheus Charming the Animals with the Sweet Accents of His Music."

In about 1570, watches started being created in distinctive shapes of crosses, flowers, skulls and animals. Called form watches, these arresting timepieces hung from the neck or waist to enhance fancy attire and were often constructed in metal or rock crystal.

There was an enormous interest in horology during the Elizabethan period which also reflected in other fields of literature and art. Christopher Marlowe's Faustus used the theme of time extensively, as do Shakespeare's plays and sonnets. From The Merry Wives of Windsor, "Better three hours too soon than a minute too late."

ENAMEL WATCHES

Art also found its way onto watch cases thanks to improvements in enameling techniques. Though opaque and translucent enamels had been used for some time to add luster and a gemstone-like appearance to surfaces, it was not until the mid-seventeenth century that the practice of painting on enamel was introduced. The process became immensely popular and was used well into the next two centuries. Part of its appeal was that it could be used for painting miniature scenes and designs on the watch case in opaque and bright colors. Earlier enamels had only been clear or transparent or, when colors were used, they were laid flat or separated. Goldsmith-enamelers and watchmakers united their talents to create a round, fairly flat watch, known as a pan or basin watch, with large surfaces to provide a broad canvas for painting floral or historical scenes. Later Louis XIV commissioned cases which featured portraits of people from contemporary history, often in allegorical form. Scenes out of the Old and New Testaments were also very popular.

Though the origins of enamel painting are largely obscure because of the anonymity of the paintings, there are some references to the craft from 1630. A reference by the artist Felicien in the "Principles of Architecture, Sculpture, Painting and all the Other Arts Dependent on Them" recounts, "Before 1630 these kinds of work were still

ABOVE

Round watch in gold, brass, and enamel. Movement signed by "F. Baronneau A Paris." France, in the middle of 17th century.

Episodes taken from the history of venus decorate this very refined enameled watch executed between 1640-1650. The enamel worker used a technique that is reminiscent of the decorative works of this period where the dominant tones are clear. This style was influenced by the famous Venitian painter Veronese and was largely adopted by French enamel painters.

OPPOSITE PAGE

Detail of "Mercury and the Three Graces," engraving by Michel Dorigny, dated 1642, after a painting by Simon Vouet.

OPPOSITE PAGE AND ABOVE

Pocket diptych sundial in ivory with garnets and emeralds France, about 1600.

Portable sundials had been in use for a very long time. Many diptych sundials were made in ivory at the end of the 16th century and in the first half of the 17th century. Best-known makers of this type of sundial were Hans Tucher, Paolus Reinmann, Leonardt and Nicolas Miller.

Diptych sundials were not only used to indicate two different types of time, but also to set the clocks and watches, whose daily variations were great, by a simple astronomic method.

BELOW

A rectangular-shaped solar watch made up of three ivory plates with numerous horizontal and vertical dials for several latitudes. Carrying a series of moon dials, a conversion from lunar hours to solar hours, and a lunar calendar, the timepiece was created and produced by the German watchmaker, Hans Tucher, at the end of the XVIth century.

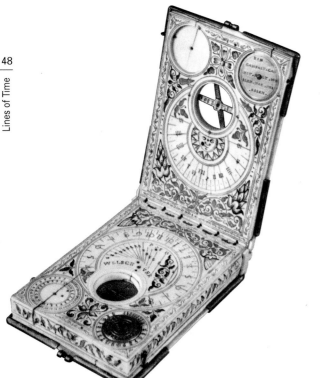

unknown, for it was only two years after that Jean Toutin, a goldsmith from Chateaudun, who enameled perfectly well with ordinary enamels and transparents and who had a certain Gribelin as his disciple, having started to search for the means of using enamels that might produce mat colors to make various hues, which might completely melt when fired and keep the same evenness and the same gloss, finally found the secret that he communicated to other workers, all of whom then contributed to rendering it more and more perfect."

Other documents confirm that by 1630 the technique was already widely used in the goldsmith-enameler's shops. Jean Toutin was established in Blois as a goldsmith in 1604, and returned to his native Chateaudun in 1609 to open a shop. Toutin is considered to be instrumental in creating, or at least furthering, the use of vitrifiable colors. Vitrifiable colors were those which could be made into glass through heat fusion, similar to the way that pottery must be fired in order for the glazes to attain their brilliance and durability. The process was an involved one, requiring many layers of application and firing between each step, and careful mixing of colors created from vegetable or mineral oxides reduced to

fine powder. This emphasis on science and technical advances continued throughout the latter half of the seventeenth century. Society was being increasingly regulated by manufactured, secularly-oriented machines, like the single microscope (invented in 1590), the telescope (in 1608), the air pump (in 1650) and the barometer (in 1643).

In 1586, Galileo observed a swinging altar lamp in the cathedral of Pisa. Having no watch, he timed the swing of the lamp against his own pulse and established the time of the pendulum's swing, finding that it varied not with the amplitude but the length of the pendulum. Huygens would use this knowledge to control the speed of the clock with a pendulum, constructing the first pendulum clock in 1656.

These technological shifts, coupled with historical events, would continue to shape the evolution of the watchmaking industry. Until around 1662, French horology was peerless. However, the emigration of many Huguenot watchmakers and goldsmiths, provoked by the revocation of the Edict of Nantes, gave a considerable boost to the industries of the countries in which they took refuge. The Huguenots established horology in cities favorable to the Reformation, such as Rouen, Sedan and La Rochelle. The watchmakers migrated to the Netherlands, to England, Geneva and Germany. Similarly, the centralization of the arts in Paris and the economic crisis and the ossification of guild regulations furthered the decline of French watchmaking to the benefit of the English.

The Stuart Restoration in 1660 also contributed to England's economic prosperity. London became an international trading center, with riches brought from the East Indies, West Africa and North America, as well as profits from industrial trades, specifically in wool and cotton manufacturing, and shipbuilding.

This trend toward England's watchmaking dominance was further aided by the discovery of the balance spring, or hair spring, in 1675 by Christian Huygens. Thomas Tompion, considered by many to be the father of English watchmaking, was the first to foresee all the improvements the invention the balance spring made possible. He conceived of a new model of watch, which became the prototype of the eighteenth century English watch, and eventually set up a shop to create a large quantity of these watches. During the reigns of Charles II, James II and William III, Tompion was the premier court horologist, and was even granted the privilege of burial in Westminster Abbey.

2

1

2

1. *An incredible Japanese clock dating from the beginning of the 18th century. Unlike the European clocks, the Japanese clocks did not indicate 12 hours for the day and 12 hours for the night, but 6 hours corresponding to the day and the night set from sunset and sunrise. To record unequal hours modified by the lengthening and shortening of the day, Japanese horologists modified the position of two weights carried by the foliot.*

2. *This automaton called the "Little Magician" was executed by Jean-David or Julien-Auguste Maillardet, in Switzerland at the beginning of the 19th century.*

OPPOSITE PAGE

Christiaan Huyens (1629-1695), portrait by G. Edelinck. Paris, Bibliothèque Nationale, Cabinet des Estampes.

New discoveries such as pierced rubies kept up the quality of English-made watches. George Graham, along with Tompion, contributed greatly to the reputation of English horology. After his admission to the Clockmaker's Company in 1695, Graham partnered with Tompion, a professional collaboration which would last until Tompion's death in 1713. The late watchmaker bequeathed his company to Graham, who was later named a member of the Royal Society Council and a master of the Clockmaker's Co. In 1725, Graham perfected the cylindrical escapement, which he introduced into each of his watches. As a last testimonial of its gratitude, England gave him the honor of being buried in Westminster Abbey, next to Tompion. The invention of the hairspring gave watch movements a precision previously impossible to reach. The decoration of watches became secondary to function. The multiple techniques that had been borrowed from jewelry, goldsmith work and enameling, were now abandoned. The greatly varied watch case forms of the first half of the seventeenth century were replaced by a somewhat austere circular shape known as the puritan watch. The emphasis shifted away from fantasy, luxury and variety of style to moderation, utilitarianism and "true" timekeeping devices.

Horological advancements in England provoked the appearance of a new type of round watch in France during the reign of Louis XIV. Its heady, bulging shape gave it the name oignon, or onion, while in England it was known as the turnip watch. Onion watches had either gilt brass or silver cases often featuring elaborate engraving on the outside. There are few extant examples of gold onion watches in part because many were likely melted down over the years for the sizable amount of metal used in their construction. There was an economic crisis during this era, and the sumptuary laws were signed, forbidding the production of luxury items. It marked the end of the Sun King's reign and the aftermath of a war, the famine of 1709-1710.

The beginning of the reign of Louis XV in 1710 signaled the start of the concentration of the fine arts in Paris. This concentration was promoted by the gathering nobility in Versailles, who formed the largest part of the watchmaking clientele. French watchmaking again flourished.

Though watches were still owned primarily by royalty, luxury took on a new meaning in this stylistic period known as the Rococo. Characterized by highly ornate and decorative designs and lines, it is a much simpler, more delicate artistic style then the grandiose Baroque period.

French watches were almost always circular, made in brass, silver or gold, and embellished with engraving, motifs and paintings on enamel. The enameling was simple, depicting landscapes of river shores, cottages and ruins, rather than the elaborate miniature paintings of people and buildings. Themes included antiquity, the pleasures of a rustic life, and love. Many watches were decorated with the allegory of love represented by rose garlands, doves, and flowery urns.

Watch dial decorations and movements were also simplified. Enamel faces were indicated by Roman numerals for the hours and Arabic numbers or tiny bars and dots for the minutes. The watchmaker's signature was sometimes painted in the center, and watches were protected with a second case covered with sharkskin or studded leather. The fashion of hanging watches from one's waist by a châtelaine appeared in approximately 1740 and continued until the nineteenth century. Men and women often wore two watches, perhaps to verify the exactness of one against the other. In his Memoirs, Casanova wrote, "In Paris, to an invitation, I wore violet satin breeches and an ash-gray coat, the ruffles of which alone were worth a thousand livres. I displayed on my chest the cross of the order; last, I took two watches and two richly chased snuffboxes."

Watches were also presented as gifts, a custom instituted by Louis XIV. On one occasion in 1681, the King gave sixteen watches to the ambassadors of Muscovy. An order of payment from the watchmaker reads: "To Baronneau, horologist, 2,489 livres for two clocks and sixteen watches which were given, to wit, to the first ambassador one clock and six watches, to his son, four watches and to the Chancellor, one clock and six watches."

French watches were fashionable, and overall, there was a tendency towards simpler styles. Indulgence encouraged the individual to gain personal enjoyment over showiness. Objects used in daily life took on importance; clothing, jewelry, furniture and trinkets were indispensable to the lifestyles of the well-to-do. French fashions spread, and the country's watchmakers became famous all over Europe for their technical and artistic prowess. However, the newfound vitality of French watchmaking was to be short-lived. In Switzerland, watch production became a flood against which few countries could compete. Its etablisseurs and division of labor meant that the company could multiply commercial outlets in Europe and the Middle and Far East. Before long, Switzerland's horological exports included Turkish watches, Chinese watches, form watches and musical watches.

ABOVE

An organ clock in wood, bronze, brass, and enamel. Dial signed Ferdinand Berthoud, Paris.

The music clock fitted with a set of flutes or a tympanum were very fashionable in the second half of the 18th century. Many watchmakers from La Chaux-de-Fond excelled in their production.

Berthoud's work was rewarded by the title of General Inspector of the Equipment of the French Navy and member of the Royal Society and the Académie des sciences.

OPPOSITE PAGE

Louis XV in 1751, a painting by Carle von Loo.

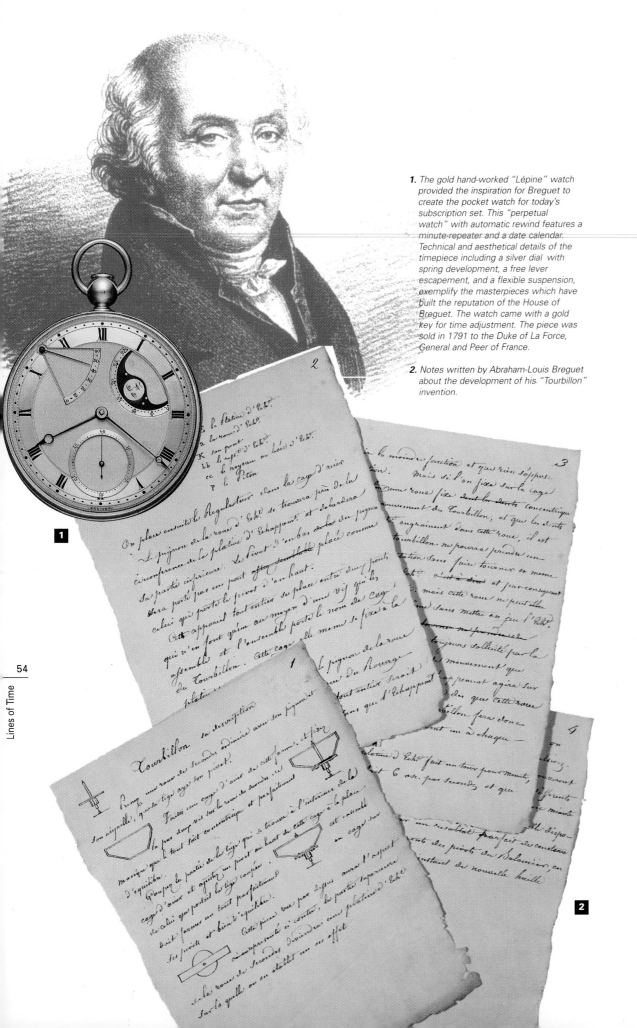

1. The gold hand-worked "Lépine" watch provided the inspiration for Breguet to create the pocket watch for today's subscription set. This "perpetual watch" with automatic rewind features a minute-repeater and a date calendar. Technical and aesthetical details of the timepiece including a silver dial with spring development, a free lever escapement, and a flexible suspension, exemplify the masterpieces which have built the reputation of the House of Breguet. The watch came with a gold key for time adjustment. The piece was sold in 1791 to the Duke of La Force, General and Peer of France.

2. Notes written by Abraham-Louis Breguet about the development of his "Tourbillon" invention.

One of Switzerland's most celebrated innovators, Abraham-Louis Breguet led a technical and aesthetic revolution in watchmaking, by abolishing the traditional engravings and ornamentation. He formed a new simplistic aesthetic, based on the components of bare wheel works. Breguet's designs were characterized by a newfound sobriety. Watch dials were made in white enamel, silver or gold. On the enamel or gold dials, hands were made in blued steel, while on silver dials they were usually gold. Breguet's watches were also notable for their extra-flat cases and harmonious proportions. The bottom and the band were smooth or decorated with an extremely fine guilloché. Breguet also used enamel on the bottom of watches built for the trade and for some of his "souscription" watches. The pendant was shaped like a ball to let the suspension ring through. Both components echo the circular shape of the watch case. Breguet's distinctive style, spread by his hundreds of "souscription" watches, would have a great influence on contemporary watchmakers.

In 1761, John Harrison further improved the precision of watches by developing the marine chronometer. His clock was one of the first timekeepers to run accurately at sea. The design, catering to mariners, earned him a 10,000 British pound prize. On a nine-week trip to Jamaica his chronograph was only five seconds off.

Around the middle of the nineteenth century, there was an important practical improvement to watches. In 1842 Adrien Philippe presented the first watches that contained a winding system. Soon after, precision watches could be fitted with a minute repeater to sound the time, a perpetual calendar indicating the date even in leap years, and a chronograph.

Perhaps no event, however, or series of events, helped change the way humans perceived time as did the Industrial Revolution. The rise and spread of the factory system during this era forced large numbers of Europeans to work in environments that were increasingly regulated by clocks and whistles. Punctuality was at a premium; tardiness was "paid for" by fines or loss of employment; and machines set the pace at which men, women, and children labored. Time became a commodity that could be "saved," "spent," or wasted. Laborers sold it; entrepreneurs bought it. Work time and leisure time were clearly demarcated, and there arose an industrial work ethic that stressed time thrift. Humans were subordinated to machines rather than natural or personal rhythms, and productivity was stressed over individual skills or expression.

New means of transportation, especially railways, helped to accelerate the pace at which Europeans lived their daily lives.

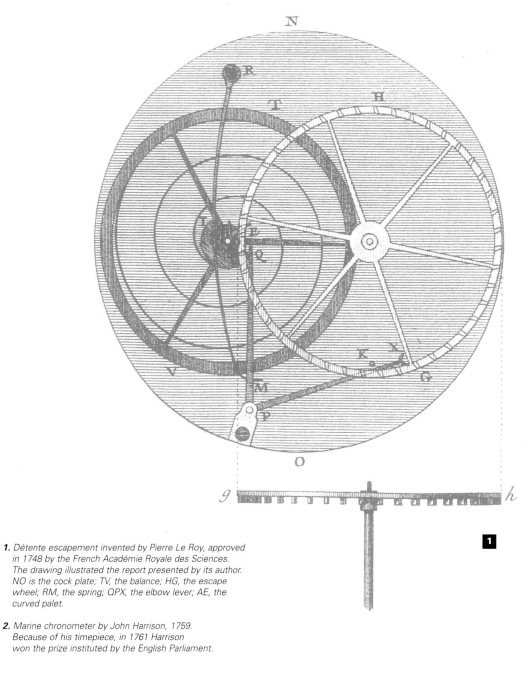

1. *Détente escapement invented by Pierre Le Roy, approved in 1748 by the French Académie Royale des Sciences. The drawing illustrated the report presented by its author. NO is the cock plate; TV, the balance; HG, the escape wheel; RM, the spring; QPX, the elbow lever; AE, the curved palet.*

2. *Marine chronometer by John Harrison, 1759. Because of his timepiece, in 1761 Harrison won the prize instituted by the English Parliament.*

1. *Watch in a shape reminiscent of a lily in gold, translucent blue enamel and diamonds and made by the manufacturers Clémence Frères of La Chaux-de-Fonds, Switzerland, during the last quarter of 19th century. Swiss watchmakers-jewelers of this period excelled in the creation of luxury watches in the shape of flowers, fruits, butter flies, beetles, rings, etc.*

2. *The spectacular Planetarium executed by François Ducommun in 1817 in La Chaux-de-Fonds and presented today at the Musée International d'Horlogerie. Made of brass, cardboard and wood, the planetarium presents the solar system as it was known at the beginning of the 19th century. The sun is surrounded by its planets and their satellites represented by silver spheres: the earth, the moon, Mercury, Venus, Mars, Jupiter, with its four satellites, Saturn and seven satellites and Uranus.*

Novelist George Whyte-Melville observed: "Ours are the screw-propeller and the flying-express — ours the thrilling wire that rings a bell in Paris even while we touch the handle in London — ours the greatest possible hurry on the least possible provocation — we ride at full speed, we drive at full speed — eat, drink, sleep, smoke, talk, and deliberate, still at full speed — make fortunes and spend them — fall in love and out of it — are married, divorced, robbed, ruined, and enriched all ventre a terre! nay, time seems to be grudged even for the last journey to our long home." Work schedules, business appointments, and railway timetables regulated the rhythm of life in industrializing societies. Inventors, investors, business managers, and efficiency experts like Frederick Taylor strove for technological and organizational advances that would render production more time-efficient and transportation and communications more rapid.

All of these changes shifted man's perception of time dramatically, making accurate timepieces a necessary part of daily life. Even religion and philosophy focused on efficiency. New religious sects like the Methodists reinforced the Calvinist notion that wasting or losing time was a sin. They urged the faithful to "walk circumspectly... saving all the time you can for the best purposes; buying up every fleeting moment out of the hands of sin and Satan." The philosopher David Hume praised incessant activity and hard work. Voltaire complained about the excessive number of religious holidays that kept laborers from their productive tasks.

The hunger for accurate timekeeping was sated by a mass production of clocks and watches. This meant that, for the first time in history, watches were affordable to the lower middle class and even some of the more highly-paid members of the working classes. Visitors of the 1889 World Exhibition witnessed the "complete transformation of work methods" in the field of horology. Fifty-five French and thirty-six Swiss exhibitors presented watch parts that could be created through new mechanical processes. In the same year, Paul Garnier, horologist for the French Navy, presented a report at the Chronometry International Congress on the changes happening in watch manufacturing: "The manufacturing by machines, or mechanical production, is being applied not only on cheap watches but on the precision watches. The perfection of the parts is such as to allow their interchange-ability." New methods were being used in the production of watch parts from springs and dials to hands and glasses.

Exhibited at the International Universal Exhibition in Paris in 1878, this masterpiece exemplifies the work of Ami LeCoultre-Piguet which was rewarded with a bronze medal. Starting from the top of the dial, are the power reserve indicator, the perpetual calendar indicating both the date and leap years, a double ring showing the hours and minutes, an hour circle for the alarm, the months, the age and the phase of the moon, the quarters of the moon, the days of the week and a thermometer.

The outer circle, indicating the minutes and the seconds, is used for the operation of the chronograph which has a counting hand to add the minutes, a sweep second-hand and a fly-back hand which also indicates the seconds.

THe movement has an automatic striking mechanism for the hours and the quarter hours. It also has a repeater for the hours, quarter hours and minutes.

This work took four years to complete.

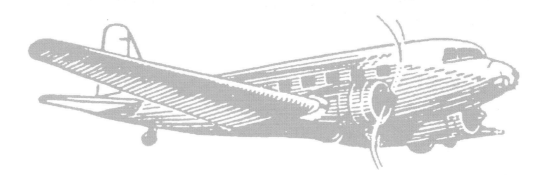

1. Symbol of the thirties, the way across the
ocean from Europe to the "new world "aboard
the sumptuously decorated cruise liners.

2. The Trapezoid watch by Cartier circa 1940.
A 14K yellow gold trapezoid-shaped case, with
black enamel geometric motifs and silvered dial.

This era also marked an experimental phase in wristwatch creation. In World War I, soldiers on both sides realized that they no longer had the time to unbutton overcoat and uniform jackets to know the time. In the early months of the war, it was reported that "not only officers, but troops in general customarily wore their watch on their left wrist." For the United States Army, Cartier developed its famous Tank wristwatch.

The first significant success of the wristwatch, however, surfaced among the female customers. Though many early watches were worn by society ladies, the spread of wristwatches grew drastically among women who worked and needed to know the time. A 1902 report from a German watchmakers' trade magazine said that "More and more women are stepping into public life, working as cashiers and clerks in post offices and schools."

The worlds of sports and transportation were also responsible for increasing the popularity of the wristwatch. One Munich wholesaler advertised in 1909 to a market of "horsemen, officers, and motorists." Similarly a business report by Hanau in 1902 noted that, "Distribution is mainly in Switzerland and France, but also in the better areas of Germany. Women are wearing wristwatches most

often for travel or sport. One also sees many men wearing them, though of course in more massive form."

Bicycles also had an effect in promoting the wristwatch. Cobblestone roads and unstarred roads in the city made it dangerous for bicyclists to pull out a pocket watch while riding. Before 1900, protective cases were created so that riders could attach their watch to the handlebars. After pocket watches started being worn on the arm, bands were created in leather and metal, with special attachments to allow a watch to be used as a pocket watch or wristwatch. After 1910, ornamental accessories were made specifically for women to allow their watches to be worn on a brooch or on the arm. Many women's pocket watches were then converted to wristwatches. The bow knob and stem was shortened, a new winding knob was fitted, the dial was turned ninety degrees, and an attachment was added for the band.

After 1915, wristwatches became the most important part of the production programs of many Swiss watchmakers. A Rolex watch was given a Class A certificate by the Kew Observatory in England for its working chronometer. In 1927, Rolex introduced the Oyster, making it famous with one of the first and

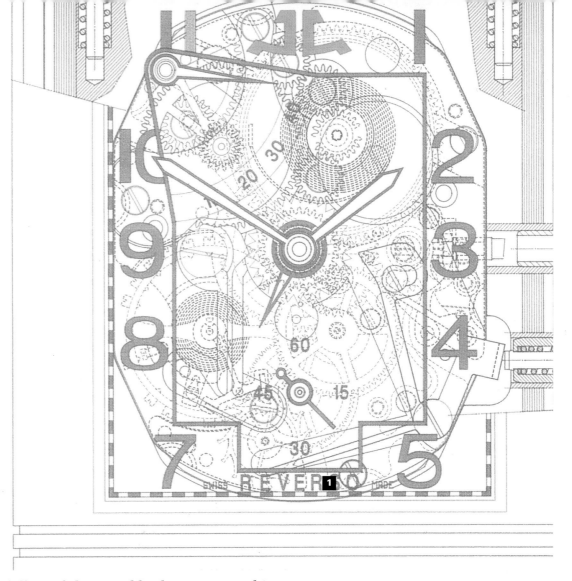

most successful advertising campaigns ever, featuring Mercedes Gleitze wearing the timepiece on her wrist as she swam the English Channel. Water-resistant watches boom in the United States doubled the initial market of the Swiss Watch Industry. As Pearl Harbor brought America into World War II, US imports of Swiss watches represented a value of about three hundred million dollars.

By 1950, over 40 million wristwatches had been produced. In 1952, France and the United States jointly announced that they were making developmental progress in the field of the electromechanical wristwatch. However, a lasting miniature battery needed to be invented first. An electric power system similar to those used in large clocks was used, and by 1957 the U.S. Hamilton watchmaking company began producing a series of electric watches. Ten years later, prototypes of quartz wristwatches achieved precision record in competition at the Neuenburg observatory. By 1970, the quartz fever has started. Max Hetzel developed the Bulova Accutron. Two million pieces were sold and numerous displays of quartz watches shown at the Basel Fair. The battery-powered watches also permitted another deviation from the century-old analog timepieces with the introduction of the digital display. The 1980's brought an avalanche of quartz watches, more than 3

billion of them worldwide, a new trend in all colors, shapes and sizes. But no trend would be as significant as the mechanical watch revival… Traditional watchmaking and its artisans not only managed to survive the quartz craze, they surpassed it. Mechanical masterpieces became the new stars of all times.

Watch specialists have taken their skills to new heights, devising ways to combine increasingly complex movements with innovative designs. In the lines of time, the next step in time starts where time will always stand still, in the heart of those who perpetuate the art of time-telling and watchmaking.

1. The watch with "two faces." The Reverso is a genuine piece of "watch crafting" Art Déco ever since it was invented in 1931.

2. A wristwatch of the seventies by Dugena. Quartz in a plastic case.

"Switzerland" brings to mind images of majestic, snow-capped mountains. Known as the "playground of Europe" for its recreational facilities, the country has seduced jet-setters and tantalized Alpinists from around the world with the lure of powder covered slopes and luxury accommodations. Similarly, for the Epicurean, Switzerland conjures world-class chocolate and cheese; and for the financier, its banks rank among the best in the world. Yet the attention given to Switzerland's mountains, culinary morsels and banking belies one of the country's most important and intriguing assets –

How few objects are still produced with such care and passion for detail! If you are interested, let's walk down the Yellow Brick Road of watch-making Switzerland: Lucerne, Zermatt and St. Moritz draw the largest annual crowds, but a more adventurous traveler can find a richer cultural experience in the traditional, horological cities of Le Brassus, Le Locle, Bienne and La Chaux-de-Fonds. Whether one is learning the basics about watches, or is a veteran timepiece collector, Switzerland is the place to go. Every Swiss watchmaking tour begins in Geneva, in the country's most southwestern corner. Geneva is

A Step in Time

a tradition of Swiss watchmaking. For nearly 400 years, Switzerland has indeed produced the highest-quality wristwatches and assorted timepieces in the world. Watchmaking is an art that requires the ultimate in creative thinking and experienced craftsmanship, all anachronistic qualities in this age of fast-paced and short attention span information. Preserving the tradition, master watchmakers continue to practice their craft on the same benches where their fathers and grand-fathers worked. Behind monocles, they put together hundreds of tiny wheels, screws and springs into the making of a single watch.

the capital of Switzerland and home to Patek Philippe, Vacheron Constantin, Chopard, Baume & Mercier, Piaget and Rolex, to name a few. One then proceeds through the Jura mountains, and eventually the tour culminates in Schaffhausen in north central Switzerland. The country's unique physical features shape its internal structure as well as the course of the tour. The entire journey spans nearly 300 miles, four languages, eight different cantons, and over 400 years of watchmaking history. Because mountains separate parts of Switzerland, each canton has its own laws and government structure.

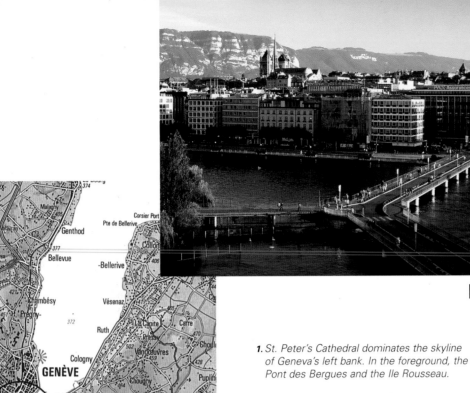

1

Because of the three bordering countries, Germany, France and Italy, people in Switzerland speak four official languages. In the regions closer to Germany, over half of the seven million Swiss inhabitants speak German; one-fifth in the West speak French; in the southern valleys, one-tenth speak Italian; and a few speak Romansch, a language of Latin descent prevalent in the center of the country. The Alps cover sixty percent of Switzerland, so while the country is quite large, one fourth of its land is unproductive, located in the high mountain areas of rock, boulders and glaciers.

1. St. Peter's Cathedral dominates the skyline of Geneva's left bank. In the foreground, the Pont des Bergues and the Ile Rousseau.

2. One of Geneva's most famous landmarks, the Jet d'Eau shoots water 500 feet high from March to October.

2

GENEVA

Most visitors enter Switzerland through a crescent-shaped area which runs along Lac Léman, or Lake Geneva, a body of water that Russian writer Fyodor Dostoyevsky once called "sublime, sparkling [and] magical." The northern part of the lake offers sunny shores and a mild climate. It is the perfect setting for grape-growing, and the region has become known for its vineyard slopes and historic wine villages. Geneva is the third largest of Switzerland's twenty six cantons, yet it is still quite small. Legend has it that Voltaire once scoffed at its diminutive size, claiming that the entire city would be powdered if he were to shake his wig!

PREVIOUS PAGE

An 18th century "Cabinotiers" workshop. The painting epitomizes Vacheron Constantin's commitment to the highest standards of craftsmanship.

What it might lack in size, Geneva makes up for with a cosmopolitan city landscape. Its bustling railway station, the Gare de Cornavin, ties the city to the rest of the world with express international connections. Geneva's Cointrin airport is served by nearly 150 airline companies. These transportation systems travel over the three mountain ranges that surround Geneva – the French Savoy Alps to the South, the Jura and Vaud Alps to the North. These mountains have been known throughout history, not only for their imposing beauty, but as a barrier for passage and transport. Before the age of modern transportation, the natural obstruction helped to create a strong, interdependent relationship between the somewhat secluded Genevese residents.

Though it has few natural resources of its own, Geneva has always been a Mecca for commerce. In Roman times the region was called "Emporium Allobrogum" after its local tribe and was renowned for its bustling fairs. Today, the city remains a world class power and the home of numerous global companies and organizations. In 1814, Geneva joined the Swiss Federation, and became the neutral meeting ground for international conferences. The city became the seat of the League of Nations, and by 1946 welcomed the United Nation's European office. Seven years later, the European Center for Nuclear Research (CERN) set

up its headquarters there. Today, Geneva also houses the World Health Organization, the International Telecommunications Union, and the International Labor Organization. Geneva, like most of Switzerland, enjoys a generally high standard of living. This wealth comes from the precision work that Swiss residents specialize in towards the manufacture of products, like machine tools, optical instruments, and, of course, watches. In fact, for every dollar spent by consumers on watches, over half of it goes to production costs in Switzerland. Last year, the country produced nearly 200 million watches and watch movements worth several billion dollars.

Yet for all its wealth, sophistication, and modern conveniences, Geneva is an old city, and archaeologists date its first settlement as early as 3000 B.C. The area of Geneva built upon a hill, known as the Vieille Cité, or Old Town, was the home of a Celtic tribe known as the Allobroges. This hill town later became a Roman stronghold, and in the first century B.C., was defended by the great Caius Julius Caesar against an attack by the Helvetti tribe. Ironically, the Helvetti later gave their name to the Roman province, a name which today appears on Swiss postage stamps.

Today, the Vieille Cité is the historic heart of Geneva. Just a short walk across the

1

2

A Step in Time

1. Founder of Patek in 1839, Antoine Norbert de Patek (1812-1877) partnered in 1845 with friend and genius watchmaker, Jean Adrien Philippe (1815-1894) to create Patek Philippe, one of the most influential Houses in watchmaking history.

2. Patek Philippe's headquarters at 41 Rue du Rhône.

ABOVE

Place du Molard, Geneva's commercial center, as depicted by H-G Lacombe in 1843.

LEFT

Documentary evidence of Vacheron Constantin's trade activities in 1755.

Pont du Mont Blanc from the main railway station, is the Musée d'Art et d'Histoire located close to the Grand-Rue, a well-preserved street packed with historic buildings. Rue du Rhône is another place to visit, the street for boutiques of the biggest names in fashion, jewelry and watches. The Jardin Anglais, or English Garden, is famous for its flower clock, a living, fragrant dial fashioned from thousands of seasonal plants and blooms. The Garden's National Monument, built in 1869, commemorates Geneva's accession to the Swiss Confederation.

St. Pierre's Cathedral, which dominates the hill, is a Gothic monument, built in the twelfth and thirteenth centuries and remodeled several times. The combination of architectural styles testifies to the cathedral's variegated history. Today, the Cathedral is most famous for being the birthplace of the Genevese Reformation. On August 8, 1535, Martin Luther and an angry Protestant mob stormed the grand Cathedral and overthrew the entire Catholic clergy. That day, Archbishop Pierre de la Baume fled in such a hurry that he forgot his watch. The timepiece, a single-hand oval with an engraved cross, is now exhibited at Geneva's Watch and Clock Museum.

Six years after De la Baume's exile, Jean Calvin came to Geneva to open the city gates for Protestant refugees like himself.

The resulting influx of people doubled the population of the city-state in the next ten years. Unknowingly, Calvin had changed the shape of Geneva's horological history. Many of his followers were jewelers and metalsmiths fleeing from France, Italy and Flanders. They brought with them materials and expertise from their homelands.

In the name of humility and religion, Calvin imposed a strict theocratic rule on Geneva, banning objects which he thought supported "popery and idolatry." This included crucifixes, chalices and jewelry. Stripped of their trade, unemployed jewelers used their skills to instead make watches with jewels, precious metals and elaborate settings. From these roots came the tradition of luxury watchmaking for which the Swiss region is famous today.

This swift growth in the watchmaking industry generated the formation of the world's first Watchmaking Guild in 1601. The Guild's eighteen rules included prayers before each meeting, signatures by master watchmakers on their wares to prove authenticity, and acceptance of a letter which stated the Guild's purpose as "[the protection] of the good name of the profession from incompetent advertisers." Some of the very earliest timepieces created under the Guild's nascent specifications are displayed today at Geneva's Musée de l'Horlogerie et de l'Emaillerie.

1

A Step in Time

1. The Girod-Vacheron's workshops in the 18th century set up at the Tour de l'Isle in 1846. The company would move its offices to 1 Quai des Moulins at the end of the century, where they remain to this day.

2. The Skeleton Tourbillon in rose gold by Vacheron Constantin, features a movement with twin series-coupled barrels. Its regulating unit, escapement and balance wheel are mounted in a tourbillon carriage which rotates on itself over one minute. The sapphire dial is inscribed with Roman numerals and features a power-reserve indicator at 12. Vacheron Constantin's skeleton tourbillon is part of a limited series of only 300 to be produced.

2

1. *Watchmaking history would be incomplete without mentioning Voltaire. In 1770, Voltaire gave asylum to a group of the city's artisans, expelled following riots in Geneva. By 1778, several hundred cabinotiers were working in Ferney.*

2. *The estate in Ferney where Voltaire founded his own watch factory. An accomplished businessman, he personally handled business correspondence and made use of his many international contacts. Although he could not quite compete with Geneva's industry, after his death in 1778, the expulsion of the "Ferney colonists" had become unthinkable.*

OPPOSITE PAGE

The entry of the Swiss into Canton Geneva on June 1, 1814, Detail by Jean Dubois (1767-1855). Ending rough times of Savoyard and Napoleonian domination, Geneva happily embraced Swiss neutrality.

In addition to Archbishop de la Baume's famous single-hand timepiece, the museum collection includes astronomical and mechanical pendulum clocks and an 1806 clock by master watchmaker Abraham-Louis Breguet. Visitors can also experience, through a recreated work room, the cramped life of the "cabinotiers," the watchmakers who assembled timepieces in attic workspaces barely the size of a cabinet. It is estimated that in 1788, approximately 1,900 cabinotiers worked in Geneva.

Another popular museum is located on the other side of the Rhône, in a small house which once belonged to French writer and philosopher François Arouet, better known as Voltaire. Voltaire named the house "Les Délices," or The Delights, in honor of the freedom he found in Geneva as compared to the French courts where he had so often quarelled with Louis XV's ministers. In Geneva, he also sought the advice of the renowned physician Tronchin to improve his poor health. The doctor gave him "eight medicines and twelve enemas" every month. Because of his "political" and physical diseases, Voltaire found Geneva to be a heavenly retreat where he could clear his mind amidst the beauty of nature.

Voltaire became fascinated by Geneva's manufactories and admired watchmakers for their erudition and frankness. Unfortunately, opinionated as he was, he also eventually clashed with Genevese nobility and moved to the rural village of Ferney, right across the French border.

In Switzerland, Voltaire would nonetheless be remembered as one of the great promoters of watchmaking. In 1770, when a group of Genevese watchmakers was banished for rioting against the government, Voltaire invited them to Ferney. He offered to create a counter-manufactory and sought high-profile customers like Catherine the Great, Empress of Russia, to purchase their watches. Voltaire's involvement expanded the popularity of watches beyond the confines of the Alpine mountain range, but did not create a strong enough force to compete with Geneva before he died in 1778.

After Voltaire left Geneva in 1765, the Genevese government purchased "Les Délices" and officially inaugurated the house as Musée Voltaire. The museum collection displays more than 20,000 books, periodicals and paintings, and nearly 300 objects, including Voltaire's own desk, manuscripts and clothing.

Voltaire was not the only one to increase the popularity of Genevese watches. Most of the evolution can be attributed to the rise of the "establisseurs," a position that combined the roles of watchmaker, broker, financier and production manager.

Part of Chopard's collection "La Vie en Rose," the magnificent "Imperiale" chronograph is made of 18K rose gold with white gold attachments, all inserted with rose and white diamonds.

BELOW

Construction drawing of Chopard's new automatic caliber LUC 1.96, with micro-rotor, two superimposed spring barrels and a micrometer regulator.

Jean-Marc Vacheron was one of these establisseurs. Under the rules of the Guild, Vacheron apprenticed for five years, then had three years to make and submit his watch. If the timepiece was approved, Vacheron would be admitted as a "master watchmaker," the highest distinction available in the watchmaking industry, and the origin of the word "masterpiece." In 1755, Vacheron's creation was approved and he took his place among the region's top "cabinotiers." His watchmaking dynasty, the oldest in the world, would outlast all others, and today Vacheron Constantin still creates old-world quality watches.

While Vacheron Constantin's historical headquarters remain at 1, Rue des Moulins on the Ile de la Cité, its main factory is located across the Arve river, in a suburb of Geneva called Carouge. Though every detail of the city had been planned by Piemont's court architects, it was never completed that way. Carouge is now home to many top watch companies, including Rolex, makers of the world's best known and largest-selling luxury watches. Here, the company assembles part of its estimated 600,000 watches a year, and then ships them to its 22 offices throughout the world. Piaget, a company famed for its "Haute Couture," jewel-encrusted watches, has its headquarters on the Route de Chêne, as does Baume & Mercier, a company praised for

both elegant luxury watches, and refined yet sporty, models.

Overcoming its geographical isolation, Switzerland finds in cosmopolitan and international Geneva a window on the world. Nest of many watch dynasties and center of Europe, Geneva is the ultimate gateway for the world of watchmaking.

LA VALLÉE DE JOUX

The journey from Geneva to the remote Vallée de Joux was very arduous for early travelers. Visitors coming from Geneva faced a long, winding road north into the Jura mountains, then upward through Europe's largest forest, before finally reaching the Marchairuz Pass at 4,748 feet. The trip is much easier these days and still very rewarding. After a final, abrupt descent, a rich green carpet unfolds across the somewhat flat Vallée de Joux. It is a unique community, once described as "the land that time forgot."

Easier to reach from the west, the valley was settled in the sixth century by the French. Legend has it that a French monk named Dom Poncet created a retreat bearing his name, in a place now known as Le Lieu. A hundred years later the original hamlet was invaded by barbarians. The Vallée would later be settled in the late 1600s by Huguenots

fleeing the intransigence and murderous bigotry of France's Roman Catholic Church.

Without these "émigrés," the Vallée de Joux would probably never have known the prosperity it enjoys today. At first, the Huguenots earned a modest income from summer farming. In the winter however, when the valley floor was covered in snow, they retreated to warm workshops to do wood, glass, stone and metal work, earning the people of this region the name "combiers," the French word for the roof under which they toiled.

Winter productivity was easy, as the valley was rich with raw material and energy sources. Workers harnessed the energy of rushing mountain streams to power saw-mills, and the region's abundant timber produced the charcoal necessary to heat metal smelters. The resulting ore was almost free of impurities and was used to make high-quality tools and knives. These precision devices were intrumental in ultimately gaining the Vallée de Joux its reputation for making excellent, high-quality timepieces.

Despite the valley's resources, many combiers left their tiny villages to secure steadier work in Geneva, the capital of Swiss watchmaking. However, as they left, others came. And, although Geneva was the center of watchmaking, the valley

Overlooking the Vallée de Joux from the "Dent de Vaulion." Upon entering the valley is the village of Le Brassus. On the right side of the lake, is Le Sentier.

ABOVE

The watchmakers at Blancpain have worked on the benches of this old farmhouse in the village of Le Brassus since 1735.

BELOW

Jéhan-Jacques Blancpain, born in 1723, founded Montres Blancpain.

was increasingly becoming known for its generations of "cadraturiers," or under-dial and dial-train specialists. They defined the region's vital watchmaking role as distributors of parts.

These distributors fought to have Geneva's stringent Guild rules relaxed. Critics argued that while the Guild's rules made sense for towns and densely populated regions like Geneva, they only served to restrict the development of smaller, remote regions like the Vallée de Joux. In 1776, they succeeded and the Guild charter was amended, leaving the valley artisans free to flourish. In the absence of these restrictions, an early form of subcontracting kicked in. Local watchmakers focused on ancillary jobs, specializing in the making of movements, under-dial work and ébauches. Their activities were very different from those of Genevese craftsmen, who set about to create an entire watch. This concentration of skills produced such quality work that nearly every watch manufacturer in Geneva came to rely on them for their movements, turning the valley into what Jean César Piguet called, in 1881, "a land of plenty where poverty was totally unknown."

La Vallée de Joux played a large role in gaining Switzerland its worldwide reputation for precision watches. The trade has lasted to this day, and the valley's watchmakers continue to work in much the same way their forefathers did, patiently handcrafting fine watches in tiny, modest rustic workshops called "ateliers."

The valley's craftsmen also earned themselves a reputation for what is known in the watch industry as "complications," mechanisms in a watch movement that perform functions other than telling time. Among these complications are the perpetual calendar, which displays the day of the month, and often the day of the week, and a self-adjusting device indicating the months' varying lengths, and even leap years; the minute repeater, which chimes the hours, quarter hours and minutes; and the tourbillon, which compensates for timing errors caused by gravity. Today, most of Switzerland's complications are still produced in La Vallée de Joux.

Of all the valley's prestigious Houses, Audemars Piguet remains a cornerstone. In 1848 Louis Audemars opened one of the valley's first factories in Le Brassus, on the Lac de Joux. There the founders began making fully finished watches in their own workshop. Today the company manufactures nearly 14,000 pieces each year, many of them featuring complicated mechanisms.

Right around the corner from Audemars Piguet, is Blancpain, a company that has come to symbolize the region's economic recovery. In the early 1980s, the company was on the verge of oblivion. Nowadays, Blancpain's position is prominent among the valley's companies, with its workshop in Le Brassus. Recently, the firm produced the "1735" to commemorate the year the company was founded. This prestigious watch holds a minute repeater, perpetual calendar, split-seconds chronograph, tourbillon, and moon-phase indicator, all in a platinum case. Only thirty of the "1735" will ever be produced. The company's philosophy highlights the spirit of its founder, Jehan-Jacques Blancpain with its now famous motto: "Since 1735, there has never been a quartz Blancpain watch. And there never will be." Blancpain also manufactures watches that revive the popular art of clockwork erotica. One of these watches, for example, displays a scene of a couple "working for posterity" with mechanical "movements" controlled by the winding of the crown. In the 17th century, history has it that Louis XV's peers showed these timepieces to young ladies to make them blush. They are now sold as valuable collectors' items.

1. The "1735" by Blancpain. An extraordinary watchmaking masterpiece combining moon-phases, perpetual calendar, tourbillon, split-seconds chronograph and minute repeater, all housed in an ultra-slim platinum case.

2. Le Brassus in the 19th century, home of Audemars Piguet, Blancpain, Breguet and many other watchmakers.

1

2

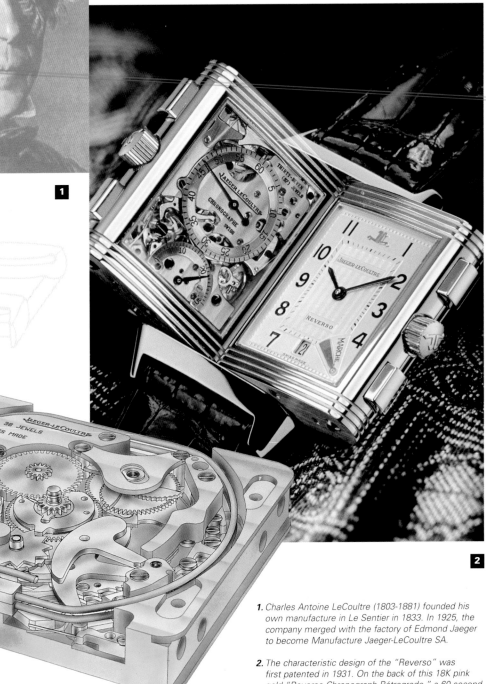

One of the largest and most impressive factories in the Vallée de Joux belongs to Jaeger-LeCoultre, on the site of the LeCoultre family's original 16th century farmhouse in Le Sentier. 25,000 watches are assembled here each year. More than half of these watches are the famous "Reverso," the "flip-over" watches originally created in 1931 for British polo players in India. The special reversible face shielded the watch crystal from breakage. Though most of today's Reverso owners aren't polo players, this innovative timepiece remains a coveted status symbol. The people at Jaeger-LeCoultre pride themselves in manufacturing each and every part in their watches, down to the last tool used to create them, contributing to the valley's worldwide reputation for its quality production.

The seemingly sleepy Vallée de Joux is home to the aristocracy of the watch industry. Among the mandatory stops is also the Hôtel de la Lande in Le Brassus. William Schmid – a former watchmaker – and his wife Micheline have lived here for nearly 35 years. Together, they run the region's most popular spot for watch industry professionals. At breakfast, guests are treated to the world's best home-made strawberry jam, and to Mr. Schmid's schedule headaches: by lunchtime, his dining room will be packed, and read like the Who's Who of the watchmaking world. How to sneak Jaeger-LeCoultre executives

1. Charles Antoine LeCoultre (1803-1881) founded his own manufacture in Le Sentier in 1833. In 1925, the company merged with the factory of Edmond Jaeger to become Manufacture Jaeger-LeCoultre SA.

2. The characteristic design of the "Reverso" was first patented in 1931. On the back of this 18K pink gold "Reverso Chronograph Rétrograde," a 60-second counter and a retrograde minute-counter over a 30 minute-period are displayed on the bottom plate of the hand-wound movement.

3. A three-dimensional CAD rendering of the Jaeger-LeCoultre caliber 943, a movement designed for the "Reverso Répétitions Minutes."

past the Audemars Piguet party, while at the same time concealing Blancpain Japanese agents from Breguet representatives? By early dinner time, Mr. Schmid will be in recovery room by the bar, savoring succulent local "saucisses," tirelessly counting tales of the valley to a few bewildered tourists.

There was a time when these valley companies were not so prosperous. In the late 1970s, employment rates were a third of what they are today. The invasion of accurate, inexpensive quartz movements coupled with a worldwide recession threatened the mechanical watchmaking industry. To counter the menace and boost its economy, Switzerland entirely overhauled its marketing strategies, creating for the first time a cohesive business plan to promote its fabled watchmaking tradition. Also instrumental in the turnaround was, ironically, the decision to make the very quartz watches which threatened them. In time however, true watch lovers returned to the rare and treasured hand-finished mechanical watches created by Swiss craftsmen. With this renewed nostalgia came a new demand for complicated mechanical watches, which translated into increased business in the Vallée de Joux. One of the companies considered pivotal in reviving the Vallée de Joux's watch industry is Patek Phillipe. The auction of its famous Calibre '89, a sale considered to be one of

watchmaking's most dramatic moments, brought about a renewed interest for the region's complicated masterpieces. Patek Phillipe's Calibre '89 took a full nine painstaking years to manufacture in an atelier outside of Le Sentier. It is widely regarded as one of the most complex watches in history, with an unbelievable total of 33 complications. On April 9, 1989, the masterpiece fetched an auction price of $3.17 million, the highest sum ever paid for a single watch.

The valley's craftsmen have worked hard to keep up with the demand for their watches. Audemars Piguet created the "Triple Complication," with a perpetual calendar, minute repeater and chronograph. Breguet unveiled an awesome line of complications, including a tourbillon, jumping hour, minute repeater and a new "souscription" set, while Jaeger-LeCoultre launched the remarkable Reverso tourbillon and minute repeater.

LE LOCLE

North of the Vallée de Joux, alongside the shimmering waters of the Lac de Joux, the Jura mountains reappear into view. Though not as dramatic as Switzerland's Alps, their distinctive limestone peaks climb 5,000 feet into the air, covered with dense groves of pines. The Jurassic Period takes its name from this mountain range, and in the winter, harsh winds and

ABOVE

Le Brassus famous "Hotel de la Lande" at the turn of the century. Although almost untouched, the stables are today the "salons" of the valley's watchmakers, and the old "Place du Marché," one of the most crowded parking lots in the region.

ABOVE

Le Locle's Clock and Watch Museum at the Château des Monts built in 1780 and previously owned by Ulysse Nardin. Among its many treasures, the "Perpetual Pocket Timer" watch by Perrelet, ébauche of the automatic movement.

A Step in Time

1. Jean-Richard is Le Locle's local hero, and his statue examining a watch still stands in front of the Post Office.

2. The "San Marco Jaquemarts" by Ulysse Nardin. The minute repeater with its animated clock work encased in platinum. Only 30 pieces were produced.

3. At the age of 23, Ulysse Nardin (1823-1876) founded the company which still bears his name.

OPPOSITE PAGE

The "Planetarium Copernicus" shows the precise astronomical positions of the sun, moon and planets. Its planet rings are cut from a meteorite found in 1896 in Greenland. Edition limited to 65 pieces.

bitter cold temperatures have earned the Jura region the nickname "Swiss Siberia."

Further on is Le Locle, in the canton of Neuchâtel, where watchmaking first came to the Jura. Local lore has it that Daniel Jean-Richard, the son of a locksmith, was given a watch to repair by an English merchant in 1690. Jean-Richard disassembled the watch, made drawings of its mechanisms, and taught himself how to reassemble the parts. Don't even think of trying this at home. He settled in Jura in 1691, and started instilling the art of watchmaking in his brothers, sons, and students.

Jean-Richard's renegade actions went against the Guild system, which was by now firmly embraced by Geneva's watchmaking community. Under the Guild system, watch production was low, prices were high, and master watchmakers in Geneva eagerly protected the secrets of their trade. Meanwhile, Jean-Richard was professing his methods of watchmaking to farmers and peasants alike. His dedicated pupils worked diligently during the long Jura winters, while watchmakers performed the final assembly. This new system, called "établissage," spread quickly throughout the region and soon, Le Locle had its own cottage industry, with skilled workers producing every watch part imaginable – from

pinions and dials, to keys and gongs. He also embraced mechanized watchmaking to increase production, making watches both more accessible and affordable to a wider clientele. To this day, Jean-Richard remains a local hero, and his statue examining a watch stands in front of the Post Office. One of his signed pocket watches can be seen at Le Locle's Clock and Watch Museum, built in 1780 on a surrounding hill for master watchmaker Samuel Du Bois. The museum accomodates one of the world's most complete assorted collection of electric, automatic and quartz watches.

Le Locle is also home to the company founded by Ulysse Nardin in 1846. After its inception, Nardin quickly became known for his complicated pocket chronographs and alarm watches. He went on to win major prestigious awards for his creations, including the Prize Medal at the 1862 World Fair. By the time his son, Paul David Nardin retired, the company had been awarded nearly 4,500 prizes and distinctions. In the 1970s however, Ulysse Nardin was hit hard by the worldwide recession and influx of quartz watches. A new owner and the creation of a unique and astronomically complex "Trilogy" of watches, designed by mechanical wizard and archaeologist Dr. Ludwig Oechslin, led to the rebirth and renewed success of the company.

1. *The "Tazio Nuvolari" by Eberhard. Bearing the name of the legendary Italian driver, this unique automatic chronograph with fly-back mechanism features a tachymetric scale engraved on a pearlized bezel.*

2. *In 1856 Constant Girard and Marie Perregaux got married and unified the firm Girard-Perregaux.*

LA CHAUX-DE-FONDS

Minutes from Le Locle is the Jura region's other watchmaking center, La Chaux-de-Fonds. There is a marked orderliness to the city. Indeed, in 1794, La Chaux-de-Fonds was almost entirely destroyed by a fire, and rebuilt according to a grid system purportedly inspired by the plan for New York City. The topography of the city is made up of nine straight avenues, including a main Avenue Léopold-Robert, named after a local artist. La Chaux-de-Fonds is also the birthplace of architect Charles Edouard Jeanneret, better known as Le Corbusier, and famous automaker Louis-Joseph Chevrolet.

In the early part of the nineteenth century, La Chaux-de-Fonds made clocks, as well as watches. A hundred years later however, watchmaking had eclipsed clockmaking as the region's primary industry. Today, La Chaux-de-Fonds is home to more than one hundred companies, including Eberhard and Girard-Perregaux, the oldest and most distinguished of these firms.

A watch lover's must is the Musée International d'Horlogerie, or Museum of Time, located at 29 Rue des Musées. Admirably methodized by French curator and author Catherine Cardinal, the partially underground museum holds one of the most impressive collections with more than 3,000 pieces, showcasing the history of time keeping, from ancient sundials to electronic time keepers.

NEUCHÂTEL

The tour continues up from La Chaux-de-Fonds to the crest of the mountain ridge, then down again to the foot of the Jura Mountains, where the French-speaking capital of "Canton de Neuchâtel" is located. It is an old city, highlighted by a castle and an old, collegiate church. Alongside Lake Neuchâtel, modern houses have been built on reclaimed land. Vineyards are laden with Chasselas grapes, and majestic yellow sandstone buildings adorn the shore of the lake.

The town also takes pride in its several museums. One of the most famous is Le Musée d'Art et d'Histoire, or Art and History Museum, housed in a century-old palace on the lake. The museum features many items made in the area, including collections of ecclesiastical silver, ceramics, and cotton-printing machines. One of the most exciting exhibits contains several antique watches created by Abraham-Louis Breguet, the city's most famous resident. Breguet was born in Neuchâtel in 1747. He is largely credited with the creation of the modern watch. Before Breguet, watches were large, heavy, thick, cumbersome instruments wound by key.

1

2

By contrast, Breguet's watches were slim, simple and elegant, qualities which continue to be hallmarks of his namesake company. Though Breguet did not actually create the automatic watch, conceptualized by Perrelet in nearby Le Locle, most people agree that he perfected it. His "perpétuelle" ran for sixty hours unattended and went for eight years without needing repair or losing time.

In 1921 Sir David L. Salomons, one of the world's foremost collectors of fine time-pieces, said, "To carry a fine Breguet watch is to feel that you have the brains of a genius in your pocket." Today, Breguet is universally recognized for his pivotal inventions. Among his creations are the Tourbillon, perpetual calendar and inde-pendent second-hand. Breguet's spirit lives on outside Neuchâtel, through Breguet Montres new manufacturing plant located in l'Abbaye, Vallée de Joux.

Neuchâtel is also home to many other watchmaking luminaries, like Remo Bertolucci, who recently relocated from the mountain town of Evilard. Bertolucci's company is best known for its "Pulchra" collection, a line of watches marked by curved bracelets, a shape inspired by the polished beach pebbles of his childhood on the coast of his native Italy.

Halfway between Neuchâtel and Bienne, in the town of Villeret, is Cartier's new ultra-modern manufacture. Founder Louis-François Cartier might have never imagined that, inside the immaculate glass walls illuminating the "Autobahn" section of Villeret, more than 350,000 luxury Cartier watches would be produced annually. Among Cartier's most recognized models, are the Santos-Dumont, the Tank and the Pasha watches introduced by the founders and still assembled today.

1. Descendants of the nautical timepieces designed by Abraham-Louis Breguet after 1815, the modern-day "Marine" line features the silvered dial, blued-steel "pomme" hands and engraved case back bearing signature of the founder design.

2. The Breguet skeletonized Tourbillon in 18K gold. Its hand-wound movement is entirely engraved by hand. The small second-hand is displayed on the tourbillon shaft.

3. Abraham-Louis Perrelet is held as the inventor of the first automatic watch in 1770. His invention meant that, at last, watches could be constantly rewound by means of natural movement. Two hundred years later, the watch automatic winding mechanism is still functioning accurately.

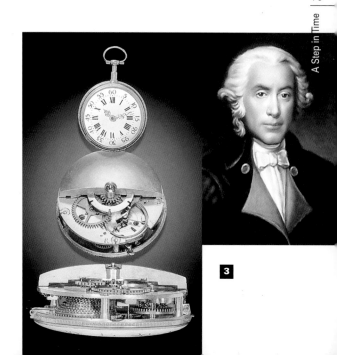

3

TAG-Heuer headquarters are also on the way from Neuchâtel to Bienne in a small town called Le Marin, north of Lake Neuchâtel. Along with Breitling, TAG-Heuer is widely credited with helping to create the chronograph craze that has swept the watch world in recent years. Founded in St. Imier in 1860, the Heuer company introduced the first stopwatch indicating 1/100 of a second in 1916. The firm became the Official Timer of the 1920, 1924, 1928 and 1980 Olympic Games. When Heuer went nearly bankrupt in the mid eighties, the company was acquired by the TAG Group and made a swift comeback as TAG-Heuer, now one of Switzerland's best-known and best-selling brands, a testimony to both its own strength and the growth of the luxury sports watch market.

BIEL or BIENNE

Just a short ride to the northeast from Neuchâtel is the fourth Swiss canton of the trip, the Canton de Bienne. Here, the city's residents are fluent in both French and German. The linguistic duality owes itself to the influx of watchmakers early in Bienne's history, from the French and German speaking areas of the Jura. The French name the region Bienne, while the Germans call it Biel.

A small lake, Lac de Bienne in French or Bielersee in German, is one of the landmarks here. On the southern tip stands St. Petersinsel, the island where Jean-Jacques Rousseau fled to after an angry mob attacked him for having unorthodox religious views. There, Rousseau found peace and solace with nature, and later wrote that nowhere else did he encounter such happiness.

Bienne too is known for its vineyards. The steep mountain slopes along the lake are one of Switzerland's prime wine-producing areas. The majority of the wine produced here, as in Neuchâtel, comes from the Chasselas grapes and is light, fruity and sparkling. Bienne's rarer, red grapes yield a Pinot Noir. Many visitors to the region enjoy a glass of wine, or take the two-hour "wine route" walk that begins in Bienne, before setting off to discover the region.

Bienne is Switzerland's ninth largest city. It was founded early in the thirteenth century and grew largely on the strength of calico printing and watchmaking, two very different industries. Initially, the number of watchmakers in the region was very small. Archives in Bienne show a 1799 document with the title: "Statement of working goldsmiths, merchants in gold and silver wares, and artisans working for the account of others, whether as pieceworkers, or by the day."

Only seven watchmakers were listed, alongside tallies for the production of 1,610 cases and 1,000 watches. Over the next fifty years, the numbers of watchmakers in Bienne increased steadily. Many emigrated from Germany. By 1856, the influence of watchmaking had doubled the population of Bienne to a record 6,000 inhabitants. Jacob Frisard settled there during this time. Specialized in making clocks with singing birds and other automata, he personally manufactured the rotating wheels, or cams, which produced the bird songs.

In 1809, his reputation was so strong that he organized an exhibition exclusively for his designs.

Surprisingly, the many watchmakers that moved to Bienne made no formal attempts to organize – like Switzerland's northern and eastern cities – into a watchmaking guild. Still, their influence on the town was strongly felt. The Council of the Commune recognized their importance and announced that watchmakers who had settled in Bienne before January 1, 1848, would be exempt from taxes for three years. Similarly, in Nidau, east of Bienne, the Communal Council freed watchmakers from communal fees and provided them with wood for fuel. Home to the Federation of the Swiss Watch Industry, the largest trade association with offices around the world, Bienne has many claims to watch fame.

BELOW

Son and grand-son of watchmakers, Jean-Jacques Rousseau fled to Bienne when a mob, angered by his unorthodox religious beliefs, tried to assault him. He found refuge in St. Peter's island.

Jean-Jacques's father, Isaac Rousseau, praticed as "cabinotier" in Geneva. A learned man, he instilled in his son the love for the Classics.

1. The Omega Speedmaster Professional.
"The first and only watch worn on the moon" was selected by NASA after passing a series of tests including extreme temperature and gravity – six blows at 40 g in six different positions.

2. The Omega Seamaster.
Originally designed in the 1930's, the watch was chosen by Jacques Mayol in 1981 when he set the world depth record without air supply at 101 meters. One striking feature of the Seamaster Professional Chronometer is its helium escape valve located at 10 o'clock which allows the gas in excess to exit on the way back to the surface.

3. An ad showing the Omega manufactory at the beginning of the century.

Bienne's Who's Who includes names such as Louis Brandt, Hans Wildorf, and many more. Born to a watchmaker in Neuchâtel's La Brèvine, Louis Brandt founded the firm that would later become Omega Watch Co. In 1848 Brandt first settled in La Chaux-de-Fonds, where he made his two sons, Louis-Paul and Charles-César, his partners. When he died in 1879, they brought the workshop to Bienne. Within a decade Omega was Switzerland's top watch companies with 600 employees, producing more than 100,000 pieces a year.

By the 1950s, Omega was one of the most recognized brands in the world. In 1958, the company was ranked the world's seventh top international advertiser; Coca Cola was number eight. Omega also had a long standing association with the Olympics as the Official Timer. Developed with the United States' NASA space program, the Omega Speedmaster Professional is the only watch that ever "set foot" on the moon. A collection of Omega timepieces can be found at the museum at 43 Rue Stampfli. Today, Omega remains one of the most successful Swiss names in the world.

Yet Omega and the Swiss watchmaking industry were not always so prosperous. While the quartz revolution and worldwide recession were toppling the ancestral Swiss watch order, morosity all but killed Bienne's industrial resources. When it comes to survival and renaissance of the identity of the Swiss watch industry, SMH is one of Bienne's most incredible success stories. Born in 1985 from the near-death experience of Switzerland's two largest watch conglomerates, SMH shook the world with its Swatch. An inexpensive, whimsical watch for everyone from 7 to 77, the Swatch will never end revealing all its faces: colorful, transparent, plastic, stainless steel, chronograph, scuba, fluorescent, beeper-equipped…, and as a final and considerate wink at hundreds of years of watch tradition, the Swatch automatic. More than a 100 million Swatches have already left the factory line in Grenchen, outside of Bienne. Today, the World. Tomorrow…

Before Swatch found its way to fame and while Bienne's two largest watch groups were having their troubles, Rolex strongly weathered the industry's ups and downs. Rolex has been consistently profitable and has grown harmoniously to its unchallenged reputation as the world's most popular luxury watch. Rolex watches are advertised upon the wrists of the rich and famous, and the adventurous. Just ask Ian Flemming: Rolex is James Bond's watch of choice after all.

Rolex founder, Hans Wilsdorf, was born in Bavaria and orphaned at an early age. At nineteen, with funds willed to him by his father, Wilsdorf moved to La Chaux-de-Fonds to learn the art of watchmaking.

In 1914, his big break came when he partnered with Bienne-based Aegler and created a wristwatch as accurate as any large marine chronometers. The timepiece was so precise that it was awarded a Class A Bulletin certifying its accuracy by the Kew Observatory in London. Rolex's reputation was born, and Wilsdorf soon began to judiciously advertise the extreme precision of his watches. Ever since, Rolex movements have been made in Bienne. Other Rolex innovations include the 1926 Oyster, considered the first truly waterproof wristwatch. Today, Bienne is somewhat monopolized by the company with five local Rolex factories.

Beyond Bienne is Grenchen, a tiny but very important watch center. An industrial town, Grenchen is home to several famous watch companies, including Movado, Swatch, and Breitling. Movado, founded in 1881, is the oldest of the three, and best known for it simple black Museum watch.

Just around the corner from Swatch gigantic factory is the stunning architecture of Breitling's headquarters. Founded in 1884 by twenty-four year old Leon Breitling, the company first opened a workshop in St. Imier where Breitling already specialized in the making of chronographs and other stopwatches. After World War I, as public interest in wristwatches and airplanes grew,

Breitling's "Old Navitimer Quantième Perpétuel." The circular slide rule built into the bezel dates from 1942 when Breitling introduced the initial design. It has since helped countless pilots and navigators to compute speeds, distances and fuel consumption figures as well as to convert miles, kilometers and knots. A limited edition, this model combines a chronograph and a perpetual calendar programmed up to the year 2100.

1

2

1. Basle's "Mittlere Brucke," its cathedral and the Rhine. Switzerland's second largest city, Basle spreads out on both sides of the Rhine, its left bank called "Grossebasel" and its flatter right bank, "Kleinbasel." Home of the first university in Switzerland, Basle is also renowned as the center of humanism where great scholars have resided: Erasmus von Rotterdam and Friedrich Nietzsche, to name of few.

2. The unique medieval architecture of the Town Hall is the theater of the annual Fastnacht Carnival, three days of high-spirited and colorful celebration.

3. Hans Wilsdorf (1881-1964) founded Rolex in 1905.

Breitling became a leading supplier of chronographs and chronometers for aircrafts. The company also produced wristwatches for pilots with dials echoing the look of a plane's instrument panel. In 1942 Breitling introduced the "Chronomat," the first wrist chronograph equipped with a logarithmic-scale so pilots could make their navigational calculations right on the wrist. Breitling's "Navitimer," introduced a decade later, immediately became the elected watch of the Aircraft Owners and Pilots Association. For all of these technical achievements, Breitling is one of today's leaders in precise and complex watches used by pilots – and all other avid fans – as the ultimate in tools of navigation and sporty elegance.

BASLE

If by train, one follows the Birs River, winding through the Jura on its way to the Rhine, joining it just outside Basle. The second largest city of Switzerland, Basle, or Bâle in French, spreads out on both sides of the Rhine.

Historically, the city was the center of the humanist movement, inspired by Erasmus von Rotterdam. Today Basle has over twenty museums, and hosts many international manifestations and several large folkloric gatherings. One of the most famous museums is the Kirschgarten Museum in the Haus zum Kirschgarten at 27 Elisabethenstrasse.

3

Located in one of the city's finest patrician houses, the museum accomodates a wide collection of pocket watches, including a small gold repeater with Rococo motifs made by Hans Jacob Meyer II, and a chronometer by Thomas Mudge, a British master watchmaker.

But when it comes to the watch traveler, Basle's primary role today is as a trading center, with the European Watch, Clock and Jewelry Fair, the annual event that professionals in the industry look forward to every Spring.

Basle was once home to the greatest concentration of master watchmakers. In the 17th century, Jakob Enderlin 's family provided a whole dynasty of watch and clock makers. One of the family members made himself known for having "demonstrated the correct forms for making good gearing" and "invented a machine for cutting the wheels of watches and clocks."

Though the number of watchmakers in Basle considerably increased during the 18th century, a large majority of them finally settled in Geneva, Bienne and Neuchâtel.

ABOVE

Basle is famous for its eight-day International Watchmaking and Jewelry Exhibition, better known as Basle Fair. Every Spring, the world's leading manufacturers fiercely compete, attempting to outdo each other with the most creative designs and technical achievements. Because of its success, the Basle Fair has been suffering from a shortage of space for many years now.

The cramped conditions at the Basle Fair have led to controversy towards the leading event in the world of watchmaking. Projects were launched for the relocation of the site in Switzerland, France or Germany, but failed, so new plans were drawn up for improvements to the existing site.

Over the next five years, the three buildings and the "Messeplatz" will be refurbished to welcome its visitors. Construction is scheduled to begin in the winter of 1996. Three years later, the new hall should be inaugurated. The tower itself will be operational for the exhibition of the year 2000.

ABOVE

An inside view of one of the plates of the "Grande Complication" reveals part of its minute repeater mechanism.

OPPOSITE PAGE

"Il Destriero Scafusia" by International Watch Company. 750 components activate 21 functions and complications, including a split-seconds chronograph, a perpetual calendar programmed to the year 2499, and a minute repeater, all coming alive with the help of a hand-wound movement with tourbillon regulator housed in a titanium carriage.

SCHAFFHAUSEN

Eastward along the Rhine is Schaffhausen, the final and most romantic destination of any watch-making tour of Switzerland. The beautiful old city founded around 1050 owes much of its success to the dam built across the Rhine by Henri Moser in 1868. The dam provided a considerable amount of energy, resulting in the flourishing of several industries in the area, including watchmaking.

Schaffhausen's watchmaking claim to fame holds in three letters: I.W.C. In 1868, American engineer Florenzo Aristo Jones came to Switzerland to set up a factory for his watch production. Jones had studied watchmaking in Boston but wanted to produce watches in Switzerland, "with the object of combining all the excellence of the American system of mechanism with the more skillful hand labor of the Swiss." Soon after his arrival, Jones met Henri Moser, who suggested that he establish his factory in Schaffhausen. The two men became partners in International Watch Company, better known as IWC, one of the first plants for the manufacture of mechanical watches in Switzerland. Hard times then fell upon IWC, forcing Jones to file for bankruptcy in 1875. IWC was taken over by Johann Rauschenback, a manufacturer who transformed the company's equipment

and operations, and got the company back on its feet. Today, IWC's reputation is at its best, partially because of the incredible success of its 1990 "Grande Complication" watch. It took IWC's craftsmen five years to create and assemble its 614 individual parts. Its functions require nine separate indicating hands. IWC's "Grande Complication" is one of the most complicated wristwatches ever made, with a chronograph, perpetual calendar, minute repeater, and moon-phases.

Many watchmaking companies owe their success to the conjunction of talent and knowledge that took place in Switzerland. It is here that centuries of watch tradition found the nurturing environment that set the highest-quality standards of craftsmanship and manufacturing. Guilds and organizations structured the education and training of the Art. Expert horologists shared their experiences with apprentices, who in turn improved upon their skills. At one point, even the famously secretive Swiss banks financially backed watch-making efforts. The will to master Time in every way, the ability to marry technical prowess and aesthetic perfection coupled with sound business ethics and a keen sense of survival have established the country's reputation as the leader in fine watchmaking. And while time waits for no one, the Swiss sons of Chronos, after 500 years, are still alive and well…

As children, we spent hours putting together red, blue, black, green and yellow blocks. Imagination flowed through our fingers, and slowly these blocks turned into spaceships, houses, cars and castles. Yet we must admit that the structures hardly resembled what we had intended them to be. Clumsily, we could only fumble with these pieces to form crude representations of familiar objects in our lives. We disassembled them and moved on to other activities, holding little sentimental value for the great castles and ships we had built. Perhaps the most important thing that we took away from the experience was a

His eye grows accustomed to the monocle and becomes an extension to his adept, unwavering hands, to perform the delicate surgery of setting the parts into a synchronized motion. The result is a complicated miniature machinery with a life that may well outlast that of its maker. To understand the miracle of this creation, one must see the operation that takes place inside the timepiece. This can be done by taking apart a watch, with little hope of putting it back together, or by flipping through the following pages, as we take it apart for you, identifying some of its most important components and illustrating its

Time in a Thousand Pieces

renewed appreciation for the art of construction. We also learned that most of us will never master the assembly process which requires intelligence, patience, skill and a steady hand. Imagine then what a feat it can be for a watchmaker to piece together a complex mechanical watch from hundreds of tiny, fragile parts. Small brass wheels, springs, jewelled buttons and glass pieces line his workbench. With amazing precision, he will take these parts and fit them together into one intricate puzzle of metal pieces. Most of his work can only be accomplished through the lens of a powerful magnifying glass.

functions and "complications." The essence of modern watchmaking is to not only indicate the time, but to reach a whole new "caliber" by creating a watch of breathtaking complexity: able to indicate the date on a perpetual calendar; to calculate lapses of time; to contain mechanisms which play an entire melody to celebrate the hour, or compensate for the effects of gravity. The genius behind these timepieces made them incredibly valuable. While we might never touch these masterpieces with our own hands, we can use our eyes to appreciate them with a new understanding of what they are made of.

Usually made to be as thin as possible, most modern pocket watches, also called open-face case, have a wider bezel opening. In most cases, the numeral 12 on the dial is still in line with the winding-shaft. This type of case, most popular before the days of the wristwatch, is still seen on watches worn on a chain, brooch, clasp or clip. Pocket watches come in numerous styles and are gaining renewed interest from renowned watch companies such as Breguet, Chopard and Eberhard.

The case of a wristwatch is obviously different: two small rods, or lugs, are attached to the wristlet and clipped in the horns on each side of the case. Most wristwatch cases are made of two or three pieces. The two-piece case consists of a combined caseband and bezel, and a back. The case back can be either snapped on, hinged or screwed on to the case. In the three-piece case, the caseband and bezel are separate.

To resist the moisture of the climate or the dust in sports activities, water-resistant and dustproof cases are increasingly used, enabling a good-quality watch to function accurately for several years without being cleaned. The dustproof case is made so the joints and openings prevent dust from entering the watch movement. If properly protected, the watch movement will last longer, while retaining its timekeeping qualities.

ABOVE

The pure line of a Chopard platinum pocket watch, with extra-slim movement and guilloché face. Note the bold design of the integrated head and neck, and the arch-shaped ring.

LEFT

Profiles of the most common caseband designs: the classic Bassine (a), the Étui (b), the Bassine with bead on glass-snap (c), the classic Demi-Bassine (d), with double bead (e), the Fillet (f), the Biseau (g), the Knife-edge (h), the Empire (i), the Directoire (j), the Baguette (k), the Bassine Lentille (m), the Square style (n), the Lentille (o) and the Punaise (p).

The angular side view of the striking octagonal shape of the Audemars Piguet Royal Oak.

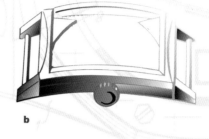

RIGHT

Basic designs of wristwatch cases: round (a), rectangular (b), three-piece case consisting of the bezel on the top, the caseband and the back case at the bottom (c), and the two-piece case made of an integrated caseband and bezel fitted into the back (d).

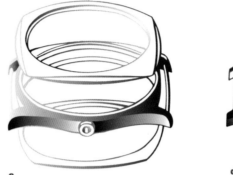

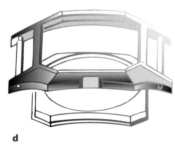

The water-resistance efficiency of a case can be tested in two ways. One is to submerge the case in a compression chamber and subject it to a pressure of three atmospheres. Once the case is removed, it is slightly warmed up. If mist forms on the glass, its water-resistance is not perfect.

The second way is to test the case by vacuum. The pressure-test does not show exactly where a watch case allows water to penetrate. If the case is placed in water over which there is a vacuum, air bubbles will come out, allowing the fault to be located.

One of the most important – though often forgotten – features of the case helps to protect the watch movement from shocks.

The earliest shock absorber was probably the "Parachute," designed by Abraham-Louis Breguet in 1790.

Obviously, knocking or dropping a watch can cause major damage to the balance staff pivots inside the watch movement. Shock-absorbing devices are usually resilient bearings designed to dampen these shocks.

If an axial shock occurs, an endstone, subject to the action of a spring, will be slightly lifted until its edges strike a fixed part of the setting and stabilize it. To absorb lateral shocks, jewel holes are fitted in the setting of several appropriate parts, allowing for a slight lateral shift, and thus limiting impact on the balance staff pivots.

THE DIAL or FACE

Among the crucial aesthetic judgment calls the watchmaker has to make, the dial or face will be the most obvious to the eye. The dial or indicating "face" of the watch is a plate made of metal or other material, bearing various markings to show all indications related to time, starting with the hours, minutes and seconds. Dials vary in styles by choice of shape, decoration and material. Indications are given by way of numerals, divisions or symbols of various types. Dials of multi-functional and complicated watches also display counters and apertures showing the date, chronographic time, power reserve and moon phases, to name a few.

The evolution of the dial is one of the most amazing accomplishments in watchmaking. In the early 1500's, dials were made of copper or brass, with large engraved Roman or Arabic numerals, sometimes both. Hours were usually indicated on two concentric circles, from I to VI and from 7 to 12, or from I to XII and from 13 to 24. In the late 17th century, Louis XIV dials were introduced. The appearance of these gilt metal dials was a major breakthrough in their design. These magnificent faces featured enamel chapters showing only the hours. Eventually, the numerals became smaller and the minutes were shown by fine strokes.

CLOCKWISE FROM TOP LEFT

The dial of a "Tank Française" by Cartier displays its recognizable white guilloché face with black Roman numerals and blued-steel "glaives" hands. The minute-circle with its bolder five-minute strokes is called "Chemin de Fer," or railway.

The "Sports Scuba" by Bvlgari. The three-part steel case frames a black dial highlighted by fluorescent Roman numerals at 12 and 6 o'clock and dot-shaped hour markers coated with tritium.

Breitling's "Old Navitimer." Four counters indicate the chronographic and perpetual calendar informations. Around its stroke minute-circle, scales allow the wearer to compute speeds, distances and fuel consumption, and to convert linear measurements.

The absolute elegance of the "Tonneau" dial by Vacheron Constantin. The 18K white gold bezel encrusted with diamonds subtly frames its silvered engine-turned dial and the twelve cabochon diamond hour-markers.

Modern metal dials are generally very thin. Colored by an electro-depositing process, they are finished with a machine-cut ornament. In fine quality dials, chapters are numerals or symbols cut out of sheet metal and stamped in relief or applied to the surface – hence called applied or *applique* markers. Dials may also feature a minute-circle to mark the minutes with a series of dots, strokes or symbols.

Enamel dials became very popular in the 17th century. They were made of thin copper or silver plates, covered with enamel and often richly ornamented. Enamel faces were comparatively thick and delicate, and were eventually superseded by metal dials. However, a sober, white enamel dial remains the mark of workmanship befitting a fine quality watch. When part of a "snap-on" dial, it is set in a fine brass ring known as the snap-ring. The ring assembly is then snapped onto the bottom plate and held in position with a set-pin.

A few companies still perpetuate the tradition of *enamel cloisonné*. This technique involves more than fifty distinct and minute steps: the making of the *cloisons*, the intricate gold wire frames shaped by hand creating individual compartments; the application of the enamel colors in each of these cells; the gentle polishing of the wires; and last but not least, the multiple baking sessions. Ulysse Nardin is among the last and most renowned Houses to master the art.

TOP ILLUSTRATION

The "Guillochage," also described as rose-engine engraving, was first designed to attenuate reflection on the dial and facilitate the reading of time. For reasons more aesthetical than practical, "guilloché" dials are extremely fashionable and the mark of fine quality watches.

Many "guilloché" patterns are displayed and combined for dial decoration. These patterns are still designated by poetic names such as "Clous de Paris," "Côtes de Genève," or "Perlage."

Dials can be carved and cut with small "guichets," also called apertures or windows. Usually displaying the date, apertures are also used for moon-phase indicators and jumping hours.

CLOCKWISE FROM TOP AND OPPOSITE PAGE

Opaque, transparent or translucent, the enamel "cloisonné" is one of the most difficult, precise and time-consuming decorative techniques.

An almost microscopic gold wire is bent by hand and applied with heat-resistant vegetable glue on a gold plate. The wire shapes the contours of the compartments called "cloisons." After a first polishing session, the inside of each "cloison" is filled with liquid enamel. The dial is then baked, so both glue and enamel will solidify. Four to five layers of enamel and twelve baking and polishing operations are necessary to obtain deep coloration and smooth finish. Ulysse Nardin is renowned for mastering this highly delicate process. Smashing models such as the "Tellurium Johannes Kepler" and its "San Marco" collection are proof.

THE GLASS

In early watchmaking practice, thin plates of glass or crystal were used to protect the dials and hands. In the 19th century, transparent synthetic materials became a substitute to natural glass: celluloid and rhodoid were first used, and then Plexiglas. Although synthetic glass is more resistant, it has the major disadvantage of turning yellow, getting scratched and less transparent in time. The glass is usually held in place by the bezel of the watch. High-end timepieces feature man-made "sapphire" glass for its clarity and elegance. Glasses come in various shapes and styles: square, round, shaped in lunette, raised, concave, beveled, in *chevé* or *Boule* style, etc.

THE CROWN

Replacing the initial winding key, the crown, or winding-button, is a knob turned by hand to wind up a watch. In the case of a hand-wound mechanism, it is fixed to the end of the winding-stem. On self-winding mechanisms, the crown will serve to adjust the minute and hour hands, and sometimes reset the date. The crown can also have a push-piece to work the mechanism of a chronograph or a sports timer, or the dome of a hunter case.

TOP TO BOTTOM

*The "Royal Oak Offshore" by Audemars Piguet.
Its unique screwed-in hexagonal crown and chronograph push-buttons are protected with custom rubber caps.*

*The "Tank Française" by Cartier.
Its delicate crown is topped by a cabochon sapphire.*

*The "Sabord" screw-in crown by Eberhard.
Exclusively patented by Eberhard & Co., this technical achievement protects the crown from shocks.*

LEFT

*The "Tourbillon Squelette" by Alain Silberstein.
Different up to the crown: the smooth opalescent triangle sapphire crown nicely complements a entirely transparent sapphire case revealing the titanium parts of the tourbillon movement.*

THE HORNS

The horns are the parts of the watch used to attach it to the wristlet, either a leather strap or a metal bracelet. Horns are usually flush with the case-band. Narrow-typed horns that are not flush with the case-band are called loops or *ailettes*.

THE LUGS, LOOPS & BARS

The lugs or loops are attachments used to fasten the wristlet to the watch. A wire loop is formed of a bent round wire soldered to the case. A flat lug is made in various shapes, cut out to attach the wristlet to the horns. On account of their shape, certain attachments are known as horn lugs.

On wristwatch cases, a thin metal rod, called bar or lug, is fixed between the horns to attach the wristlet. It may be either a fixed lug soldered to the horns, or a spring lug fitted in one of two ways: by means of two pins which stick out at either end of a hollow bar and enter the two holes of the horn. One pin is solid while the other is attached to a spring, so it will fit into the space between the horns. This is called the male lug and is similar to the attachment used to fit toilet paper into a dispenser. The other method fits the holes of each bar into the pins on the horns. A piston, set in one of the holes, is pushed out by a spring inside the bar. This is called the female lug.

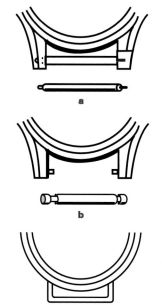

ABOVE

"Impériale Chronograph" by Chopard. Specially designed, the attachments are enhanced with cabochon rubies to match the red of the bracelet.

LEFT

On a male lug (a), the pins on each side of the lug fit into the holes of the horns. One of the pins is pushed outwards by a spring inside the lug.

The female lug (b) has a hole on each side instead of a pin. On the left side of the lug, a small hollow rod is visible. It is also pushed outwards by a spring. This time the pins are on the horns.

The wire loop (c) is formed of a bent round wire soldered to the case. The wristlet will be fitted around the loop.

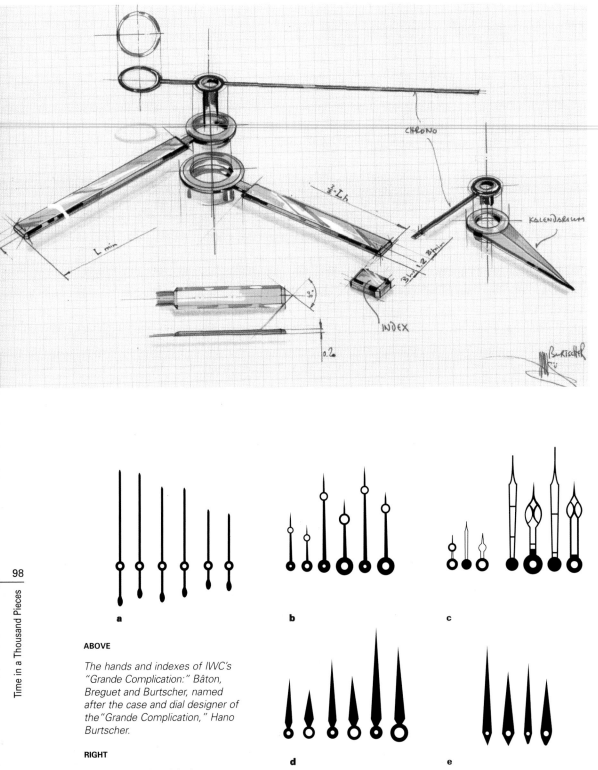

HANDS and HAND-SETTING

On the face of the watch are the indicating hands, usually made of a thin, light piece of metal, in various forms, which move over a graduated dial or scale. Watches usually have three of these hands to show the hours, minutes and seconds, but the more complicated the watch, the more hands will be displayed.

Earlier watches only had an hour-hand. Daniel Quare of England is believed to have introduced the minute-hand around 1691, although it was not generally used until the early 18th century. Because there was no glass to protect the dial, the first hands were strong and heavy.

In the late 18th century, they became more slender and were made by hand, with a file and graver. Holes were cut out in turns with a bow and ferrule. In 1764, archives show that hands were cut from a strip of metal with a punch and hammer. In the early 1800s, they were stamped out in a fly-press, often to be adorned with precious stones.

Modern hands are turned out in a great and always evolving variety of styles, qualities and colors. High grade hands are often made of tempered steel and have a polished pipe or head. They are named after their shape, and sometimes fancy ones are devised by the manufacturers.

ABOVE

The hands and indexes of IWC's "Grande Complication:" Bâton, Breguet and Burtscher, named after the case and dial designer of the "Grande Complication," Hano Burtscher.

RIGHT

Among many hand designs, the "Grande Seconde Poire" (a), the "Breguet Corps Droit" (b), the "Skeleton" (c), the "Alpha Pleine" (d), and the "Dauphine" (e).

Today, classic hands are still named after a particular style – Louis XV or Louis XVI – or after their creators – Breguet or Roskopf.

Geometrical shapes are characteristic of the modern hand design. To accommodate new trends and requirements, watchmakers have modified and adapted classical designs into innovative sharp silhouettes, like Rolex and their now famous "Mercedes" tritium-treated fluorescent hour-hand or Alain Silberstein's colorful "serpentine" second-hand. Hands cut out in the middle are called skeleton hands. When the openings are filled with a paste that glows in the dark, they are called luminous or radium hands.

The second-hand is a skinnier hand fixed to the fourth wheel. When mounted in the center of the dial, the second-hand is called a sweep second-hand or *trotteuse*.

Hand-setting is the term used by watchmakers for the operation of correcting the position of the hands. It also refers to the mechanism performing it: the hand-setting system allows to manually set the hour and minute hands at the correct time.

Originally, the hands had to be pushed directly by hand to adjust them; later, the hand-setting system allowed the simple use of a key. This operation is now easily executed with the pull-out crown, which is also – how convenient – the winding crown.

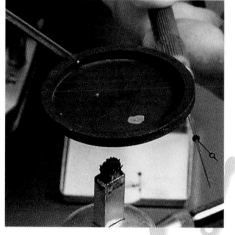

ABOVE

The delicate "blueing" operation. The finely cut and polished steel "Breguet" hands are carefully heated. Because of oxidation, their surfaces become successively light-yellow, copper-colored, brown and finally blue.

Mostly used for steel hands, the "blueing" process is also frequently adopted "to give springs a blue temper." The desired blued color will vary depending on the heat: 290° C. for a dark blue and 330° C. for a light blue.

ABOVE

Breguet's watch hands are fitted manually, an operation which requires an exceptionally precise and steady hand.

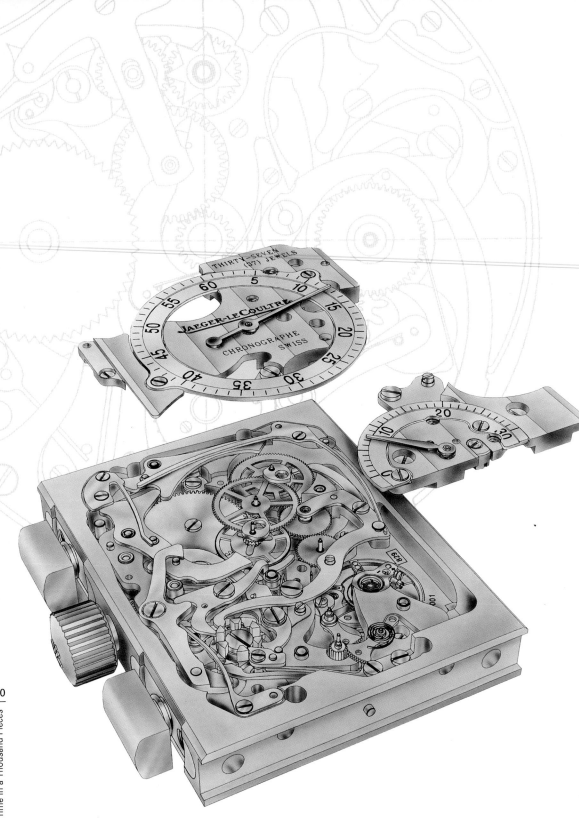

ABOVE

An exploded view of the Jaeger-LeCoultre Caliber 829, movement of its "Reverso Retrograde Chronograph" with 60-seconds counter and 30-minutes retrograde counter.

THE MOVEMENT

Now that we are somewhat familiar with the basic parts of the watch's exterior, let's open up the case to examine the movement. However, before attempting to do so, it is relevant to first understand how the watch was put together. To understand how the watch was closed is more than useful when it comes to opening it.

The back may have been screwed on, snapped on, or in rare cases, hinged to the case. The screwed on type can be identified by the slots or by a series of flat cuts on the edge. The edge may also be knurled to enable the back to be unscrewed by hand pressure only.

On the other hand, a snap-on case will show a shallow groove on its edge. In this instance, a knife blade may be used to open the case. Still, great care needs to be exercised: the knife can slip and disfigure the finish; damage can be caused to the edge of the snap; also, joints might get bruised. In a word, it is wise to let a professional handle the operation. Revealing the movement, the watch case is now open.

The term "movement" applies to the complete watch without the case. It consists of a train of wheels with power at one end to drive them, and a device to control their speed at the other end. The motion work and the hands will be added to register the wheel train speed on a dial.

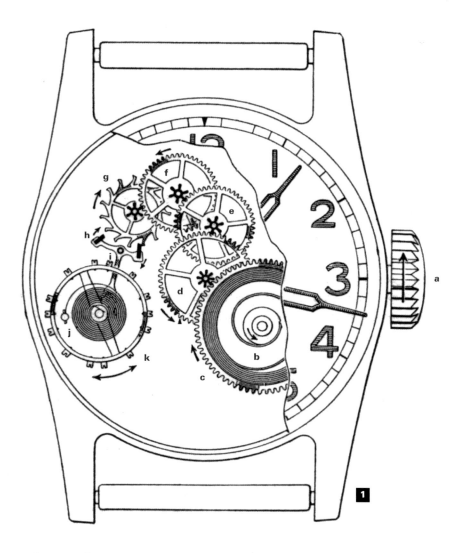

A mechanical watch movement of high quality is necessarily complicated. Hundreds of parts are used, each one cut and fashioned by skilled craftsmen. Some of these parts are so small they have to be seen under a powerful magnifying glass so that their perfection of design and manufacture can be fully appreciated.

CALIBERS

Confusion is made between "movement" and "caliber." Caliber actually qualifies the size of the movement. It is designated by the casing diameter in *lignes* or lines, and often translated in millimeters at a scale of 1 line for 2.255 millimeters, i.e. less than 1/10 of an inch. For example, a 10 1/2"

round caliber will be 23.7 mm in diameter. The term "caliber" has been used to indicate the shape of the movement and its bars, the origin of the watch, the designer's name, etc. Round calibers are the most common. Shaped calibers refer to movements of all shapes except round: oval, rectangular with cut corners, tonneau and baguette, for example.

BARS

According to the shape and arrangement of the bars, one may distinguish between various shapes of calibers: the bar caliber, in which each element of the train has its own bar; the revolver caliber, in which the barrel-bar looks like a pistol; the curved-

1. A basic watch movement in action:
The action of winding the crown (a) causes the barrel-arbor to rotate and its inner coiled mainspring (b) to wind around it. As the mainspring unwinds itself, the transmission wheel (c) – also called main wheel – rotates, transmitting power to the wheel train: first, by meshing with the pinion of the center wheel (d) which in turn meshes with the third wheel (e), meshing then with the fourth wheel (f).

The wheel train transmits the driving power to the escapement - the regulator of the movement. Controlling the speed of the wheel train, the escape wheel (g) is itself controlled by the balance (k) through the lever (i) fitted with two pallets (h). When one of the pallets meshes with the escape wheel, the lever is pushed sideways and transmits a small impulse to the balance which contains its own motion power through its hairspring (j).

2. Exploded view of a basic movement.

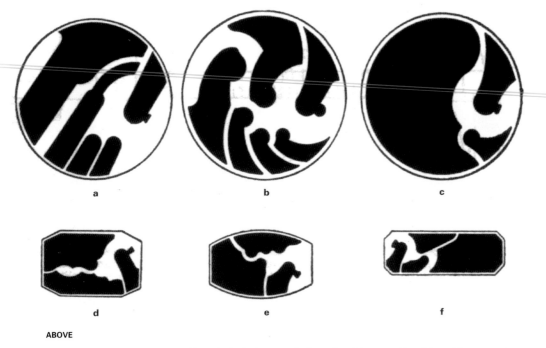

a   b   c

d   e   f

ABOVE

The different types of round calibers include the so-called revolver (a), curved-bar (b), and three-quarter plate (c). Shaped calibers can be formed in almost any configurations: rectangular with cut corners (d), the "tonneau" (e), and the "baguette" (f), to name a few.

BELOW

The winding mechanism of a manual mechanical movement. The winding crown is screwed on the outside end of the winding stem (a). On its other end, the stem is fitted with the crown wheel (b). As the crown wheel meshes with the transmission wheel (c), it drives the ratchet wheel (e). Fixed to the center arbor (d) of the barrel (f), the ratchet wheel through the action of winding the watch will cause the arbor to rotate and wind the inner coiled mainspring contained in the barrel.

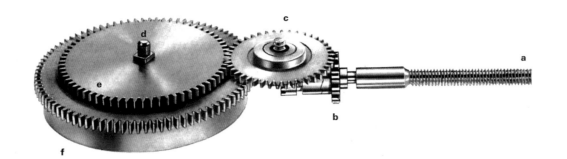

bar caliber, in which the bars curve towards the center of the movement; also the three-quarter plate, in which the entire train, with the exception of the escape-wheel, is housed under a bridge covering about three quarters of the movement surface. A few prestigious watchmakers, Patek or Vacheron for example, have given their names to particular calibers.

Nowadays, the term caliber refers less to the shape and lay-out of the bars than to the characteristic features of the design of the watch. A "good" caliber is laid out to accommodate a large mainspring and a large balance – one with a high moment of inertia – or to house movements of small diameter and reduced height.

Mechanical movements are now mostly categorized by their winding mechanisms which provide the energy for the motion work: hand-wound or self-winding, also called automatic.

WINDING MECHANISMS

Early watches were supplied with a separate key, and were wound through a hole in the back. Fortunately modern watches are keyless. In hand-wound movements, the key has been replaced by a crown attached to a stem fitted to the winding mechanism.

In hand-wound watches, the action of turning the winding crown clockwise winds a spring called mainspring, which causes the barrel arbor to rotate and the inner end of the mainspring to wind itself around the arbor.

In the self-winding or automatic type, the action of moving one's wrist causes a weight, called the rotor, to swing, winding the mainspring. Overwinding is prevented by a clipping clutch mechanism.

There are three methods of using the mainspring to drive the wheel train and they are known as the *fusée*, the going barrel, and the stationary barrel.

FUSÉE,
GOING and STATIONARY BARREL

The time-keeping accuracy of old watches was affected by the drop in power when the mainspring slackened, so a means of compensation was necessary. This was accomplished by the introduction of the *fusée*.

A cone-shaped pulley was positioned next to the barrel. The pulley had a spiral groove machined on its face in which a chain was placed. One end of the chain was hooked to the base of the cone and the other end to the outer face of the barrel side. Gear teeth were cut on the bottom edge of the cone and formed the main wheel. When the mainspring was wound, the chain pulled on the smallest diameter of the cone with minimum leverage.

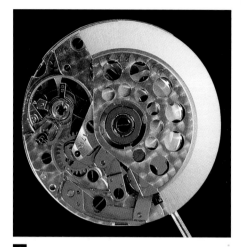

ABOVE

An automatic movement in the making. The rotor is clearly visible on the left half of the movement.

1. An automatic movement with its pierced gold rotor by Alain Silberstein.

2. The back of the 18K gold "Pasha" minute repeater and perpetual calendar by Cartier. Each of the 653 parts of this automatic movement is hand-finished. The transparent caseback allows one to admire the engraved gold rotor with its chiselled Cartier logo. This model takes 300 hours to assemble and only five examples are produced each year.

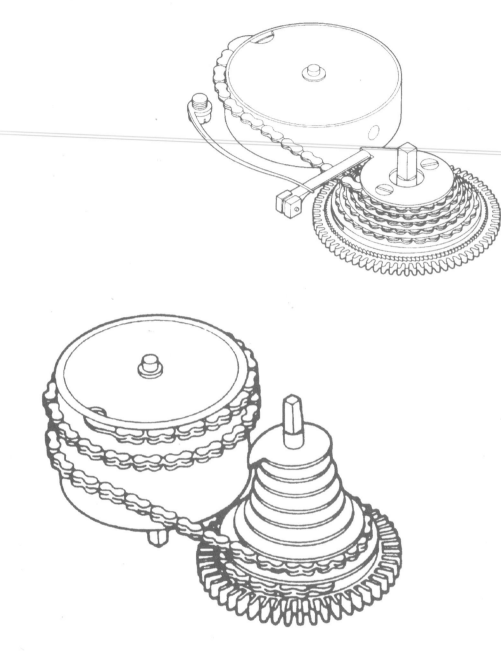

As the spring unwound itself and the power progressively weakened, the chain was being transferred from the fusée and was winding itself around the barrel. This caused the chain to pull on the ever increasing diameter of the cone with a proportionate increase of leverage. This method provided suitable compensation.

With the second method, the *going barrel* is made of a disc with gear teeth cut on the outer edge of the barrel, also named main wheel. The barrel turns freely on an arbor and contains the mainspring, hooked to the barrel at the outer end, and to the arbor at its inner end. The teeth of the barrel mesh with the first pinion of the watch train. During the process of winding the mainspring, the tension is held by a ratchet, also called the clickwork.

Finally, in a system found primarily in American watches, the barrel remains *stationary* while the arbor revolves in the center allowing the mainspring attached on its inner end to unwind.

Other essential parts of the movement include the ratchet-wheel and transmission-wheel which meshes with the winding-pinion of the train. The train, consisting of wheels riveted to their pinions, transmits the driving power to the escapement. The regulating organ of the movement is the balance with its spring affixed to the balance staff.

The "Fusée" mechanism:

*1.*When the mainspring is wound up, the chain is around the cone-shaped pulley.

*2.*As the mainspring unwinds, the chain wraps itself around the barrel. The ever increasing diameter of the pulley makes up for the loss of power of the unwinding mainspring, thus giving consistent drive to the movement.

TOUT POUR L'EXPORTATION

ASSORTIMENTS À ANCRE

L. JEANNERET-WESPY

SOCIÉTÉ ANONYME

LA CHAUX-DE-FONDS

This device is like a mechanical oscillator. It receives from the escapement the impulses required to make it run for about 24 hours, with a safety-margin of 10 to 12 hours.

The mainspring, main wheel, wheel train, escapement and balance systems form the core of the watch movement. The timepiece will also include the winding and setting mechanisms, as well as related organs, i.e. dial, hands and any other indicators.

All the movement's parts are supported by the frame, composed of the bottom plate and bars. The hands are set in motion through a steel cannon pinion, an hour wheel and a minute wheel. The cannon pinion drives the minute wheel while the minute wheel pinion drives the hour wheel freely revolving around the cannon pinion.

The hour-hand is fitted on top of the hour wheel pipe while the minute hand is fitted over the end of the cannon pinion. The gear ratios are calculated so that the hour wheel will revolve once every twelve revolutions of the cannon pinion.

THE WHEEL TRAIN

The energy stored in the mainspring serves to activate the wheel train. First, the teeth of the main wheel mesh

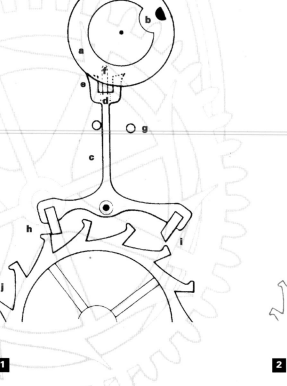

1

2   a   b   c   d

1. *The escapement lever:*
   The balance roller, also called impulse roller (a),
   is fitted with the ruby impulse pin (b) and rests
   on the lever (c). The upper part of the lever
   consists of the fork or notch (d) with its two
   horns (e) and the center guard pin (f). On each
   side of the lever are the banking pins (g). On
   the lower part of the lever are the entry pallet
   on the left (h) and the exit pallet on the right (i),
   controlling the rotation of the escape wheel (j).

2. *The four phases of the escapement cycle:*
   a) At rest, the escape wheel tooth hits the
   locking face of the entry pallet .
   b) When the impulse pin enters the fork of the
   lever and moves it away from the banking pin,
   it causes the entry pallet to be pulled away
   from the escape wheel, thus releasing the
   escape wheel tooth.
   c) Continuing to rotate, the balance roller and its
   pin push the lever further. As the adjacent
   tooth strikes the exit pallet, the lever is held
   against the other banking pin.
   d) The balance roller completes its swing and
   reverses direction. Its pin re-enters the notch in
   the lever. The exit pallet is pulled away from
   the escape wheel tooth now freed. This
   impulse transmitted through the lever gives a
   further swing to the balance. The cycle is
   then repeated in the opposite direction.

with the leaves of the center wheel pinion. In turn, the center wheel meshes with the third wheel pinion, the third wheel with the fourth wheel pinion, and the fourth wheel with the escape wheel pinion.

The center wheel rotates once every hour and carries the minute hand. The fourth wheel rotates once every minute and so supports the seconds hand.

Because the teeth of the main wheel meshing with the center wheel pinion are only a means of transmitting power to the train of wheels, timing is calculated from the center wheel.

THE ESCAPEMENT

The escapement regulates the speed of the wheel train by maintaining the oscillations of the balance. It consists of an escape wheel, a lever and a balance.

The escape wheel is controlled by the balance through the lever. One end of the lever is fitted with two pallets allowing the escape wheel to revolve one tooth at a time. When a tooth of the escape wheel comes into contact with one of the pallets, that end of the lever is pushed sideways which causes the other end to transmit a small impulse to the balance. Each time the escape wheel moves, it creates a small impulse that prevents the balance from

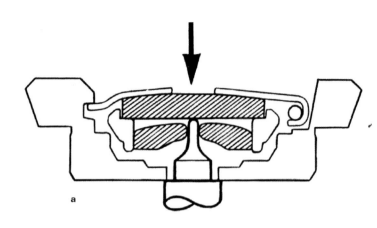

a

b

1

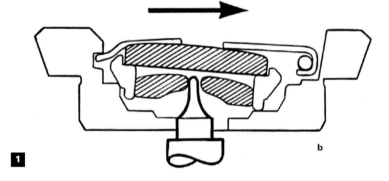

2

3

slowing down and stopping. The wheel train therefore moves in a series of jumps. To ensure sustained accuracy in timekeeping, each part of the movement must be finished with precision, all pivots polished, all friction surfaces adequately lubricated.

Everything must be done to reduce these frictions to a minimum. So-called jewels are fitted as pivot bearings for the wheels. These jewels derive their name from the time when watchmakers used rubies. The number of jewels varies with the quality of the movement and is usually 7, 15, 17 or 21. A seven-jewel movement generally indicates that only the escapement is fitted with jewels. However, a masterpiece such as IWC's "Grande Complication" holds as many as 68 rubies. While the use of rubies as bearings for the various train-arbors dates as far back as the 1700s, synthetic rubies have been almost exclusively used since first manufactured by Verneuil in 1902.

When used as caps for the balance wheel pivot bearings, jewels are then known as endstones. After the movement has been oiled, jewels and endstones retain the oil by capillary action. The escapement is fitted between the wheel train and the balance system. Both the escapement and the train are supported by two plates known as the bottom plate – beneath the dial – and the top plate.

1. Sketches of a shock proofing device illustrating (a) axial and (b) radial shocks. The device described here is a Kif Flector.
When shocked, the balance wheel is displaced, and its pivot carries away the mobile jewel in-setting and the end-stone. The shock is cushioned by the part of the staff or the arbor hitting the block. After the shock the spring brings the assembly back to its normal position.

2 & 3. The red rubies used as bearings to avoid friction on moving parts of a Breguet (2) and Vacheron Constantin (3) movements. A usual number is 17, but can go up to more than 60 on some masterpieces.

A balance wheel with its screws allowing adjustment of the moment of inertia.

BELOW

Fitting the balance spring on the balance wheel. The strength of the spring is first tested by checking that the number of vibrations it commands to the wheel in 60 seconds corresponds to the number of vibrations calculated for the gear train.

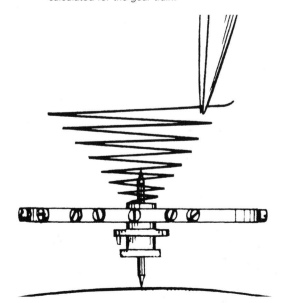

THE BALANCE

Part of the escapement, the balance is the device which, by the oscillations of its inner spring, called balance spring or hairspring, regularizes the movement of the wheel train. It is the equivalent of a pendulum for the clock.

In 1675, C. Huygens invented the flat balance spring to complement the balance. Made of copper or iron, it only had a few coils. Though imperfect, it gave the balance what it needed to become as accurate as the pendulum of a clock. The drawback of the flat balance spring, fixed to the collet and the stud, was that it developed eccentrically during its expansion and contraction. This progressively increased pressure on the pivots, causing the rate to vary. Several years later, Abraham-Louis Breguet designed an improved system in which the outer coil of the spring was raised. This new shape, called the *Breguet overcoil* ensured the concentric development of the balance spring.

The balance itself can be either mono or bimetallic. When plain or monometallic, the balance is an uncut ring made of a single metal, coupled with the compensating balance spring. The balance should need no compensating effect on its inner spring, since the elasticity of the spring itself is hardly affected by changes of temperature.

The screws on the rim of the plain balance not only enhance its appearance, but most of all facilitate the adjustment of the moment of inertia.

In a bimetallic balance, also called compensation balance, the rim is made of two metals of different expansivity – for example steel and brass – soldered together. The rim slightly opens when the temperature falls and closes when the temperature rises. The moment of inertia will be modified, compensating the effect of temperature on the elasticity of the spring, which is usually made of steel. The removable screws on the rim enable the degree of compensation to be adjusted.

In making balance springs, the most varied materials have been used, e.g. iron, copper, steel, gold, etc. Hardened steel is widely used for its valuable elastic properties. However, since steel is magnetic, subject to oxidization, and because it has a high temperature coefficient, the balance spring does require a compensation balance.

The balance mechanism in a watch must, as a rule, make a definite and invariable number of vibrations in one hour: around 18,000 for standard mechanisms, 28,800 for high-end movements, and up to 360,000 for elaborated sports timers. Many have spent time and energy trying to perfect this crucial element, quintessential in a consistently sustained accuracy in time keeping.

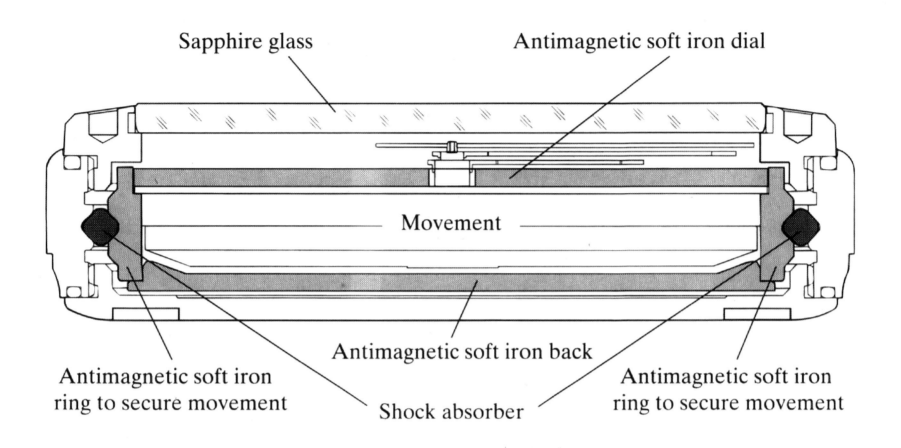

Sapphire glass

Antimagnetic soft iron dial

Movement

Antimagnetic soft iron ring to secure movement

Antimagnetic soft iron back

Shock absorber

Antimagnetic soft iron ring to secure movement

NON-MAGNETIC WATCHES

When we were kids and got bored in class, we played with our ruler, rubbing it against the inside of the arm, then trying to pick up little pieces of paper by moving the ruler above them. What we did was in fact to charge the ruler with a tiny shot of electricity, thus creating a magnetic field. That ruler was in fact some sort of magnet.

Magnetism is due to circulating electric currents. The earth itself is a gigantic magnet. We are actually surrounded by all kinds of magnetic fields. Among the most obvious are those created by power appliances like televisions, stereos, computers, etc.

Disruptions in those magnetic fields translate into the annoying "statics."

Watches contain hundreds of moving parts made of steel, their motion subjected to the laws of gravity and kinetics. While these principles are constant and thus predictable, magnetic fields fluctuations are beyond our control. If a magnet approaches the watch, its steel moving parts – the balance for instance – will be attracted to it, altering its normal oscillations.

To counter this magnetic inconvenience, watchmakers came up with a solution: insulating the movement in a jacket that conducts magnetic fields.

FUNCTIONS and COMPLICATIONS

Obviously, the primary function of a watch is to tell time. After browsing through the basics of a mechanical movement, this supposedly simple function already appears to be quite a deal, even for the brain of a rocket scientist. So, while we will not yet risk going into "complicated" mechanisms, we can nevertheless make an attempt at clarifying what complicated watches are, how they are categorized, and most of all explain what the crowds of hands, counters, push-buttons and other subdials are designed for, and their applications. Before getting into details, it is important to first distinguish the time keeping functions from the watch complications and others "complicated" features, often inaccurately qualified as complications themselves. These include a number of mechanical devices and aesthetic schemes so spectacular that confusion can occur. They feature non-horological functions such as the barometer or the altimeter, or additional mechanisms, such as the power reserve indicator, the alarm, or the Tourbillon. However, the Tourbillon is widely considered to be a "complication," if not *the* ultimate Complication.

Horological functions have pure indicative time-keeping purposes, such as the hour, minute and second, in one or several time zones.

"Complications" watches can be divided in three categories: watches with one or more additional hands – jumping seconds on a separate sub-dial, independent seconds, chronograph or split-seconds chronograph, also called chronograph *rattrapante*; watches with a repeater – striking quarters, five-minutes, minutes at the command of a push button, and the Grande Sonnerie, which automatically strikes hours and quarters, and repeats hours, quarters and minutes at command; and finally, watches with astronomical indications – moon phases, Quantième, perpetual calendar, and the Equation of Time.

This classification, while in accordance with strict watchmaking rules, omits to mention many other increasingly popular features which are sources of confusion – for example, chronometer versus chronograph – or curiosity – with the GMT, the tachometer, the telemeter, the pulsimeter and the Jumping Hour.

HOURS, MINUTES and SWEEP-SECONDS

As simple as it may appear, there are several refined distinctions to be considered even when it comes to read time. If everybody knows that the hour is read on the small hand and the minute on the long one, the seconds present several reading options. The sweep-seconds hand, or

1

2

3

1. *Jaeger-LeCoultre "Master Géographique."*
By turning the city indicator, the time of
another time zone can be read on the
subdial directly above the aperture. The day
and night indicator is at 9 o'clock on this
same subdial.

2. *Breguet "Universal Time" with indication of*
24 time zones. The base of the winding
crown allows selection of the desired time
zone setting.

3. *Audemars Piguet "Dual Time." Local time in*
the second time zone can be read on the
subdial at 6 o'clock.

OPPOSITE PAGE

Jaeger-LeCoultre's "Master Géographique" in
its entire splendor.

trotteuse, mounted at the center of the main dial, is the most common. The jumping seconds, or *foudroyante*, jumps 4 or 5 times per second and can be read on a sub-dial. The independent seconds, or *seconde morte*, is a large second-hand mounted at the center of the dial. It beats every second and can be stopped without stopping the other hands.

TIME ZONES and WORLD TIME WATCHES

Quantifying passing time however, was not at all sufficient for the modern world. The need for time zones first emerged from the scheduling problems for transcontinental railway travels. In 1880, engineer Sanford Flemming suggested that the world should be divided into twenty four time zones. Each zone, comprised between two meridians, would be worth one hour. The system was implemented three years later. Zone 0 is based on the Greenwich meridian, outside London. Time is calculated based on the G.M.T., short for *Greenwich Mean Time*, hours being added when traveling East, and subtracted when traveling West.

The principle of a time-zone movement seems quite simple. In the case of a dual time watch, the indication of the second time zone can be read on a sub-dial, by means of an additional hand, or through an aperture. When it comes to World Timers, also called G.M.T. watches, a rotating disk or interior

Time in a Thousand Pieces

bezel is engraved with the name of one of the cities from each of the twenty-four zones. Usually, an extra hand, disk or dial will track the time of the chosen time zone.

DAY, DATE and CALENDAR

When it comes to the indication of the date, many bodies of conventions have been adopted to determine the subdivisions of a year into months, weeks and days.

In past centuries, various calendars have been devised on account of the length of the year, amounting to 365.2422 days, i.e. exactly 365 days, 5 hours, 48 minutes and 45 seconds. Though very complicated calendars have been adopted, the perfect calendar, one that divides perfectly and will never have to be adjusted, has still not been created. The chief calendars may be divided into two classes: lunar calendars like the Jewish and Muslim calendars, and solar calendars.

In the Egyptian calendar from 4236 B.C., the year had 360 days divided into twelve months of 30 days each. Five extra days were added, making a year of 365 days. Still about a quarter of a day short...

In 46 B.C. Julius Caesar fixed the year at 365.25 days, with a leap year of 366 days, or bissextile year, every four years. The Julian calendar was adopted by the

Church in 325 A.D., but there was still a loss of 0.0078 day per year.

In 1582, Pope Gregory XIII corrected this error with the Gregorian calendar. He provided for the suppression of a leap year every hundred years, with the exception of years whose numbers are divisible by 400. 1700, 1800 and 1900 were not leap years, but 2000 and 2400 will be. The Gregorian calendar was adopted by Catholic countries in 1582, followed by the Protestant States of Germany and by Denmark in 1700, Great Britain and its possessions, including North America in 1752, by Japan in 1873, by China in 1912, by Russia and by other orthodox countries of Europe as late as 1940. However, the Gregorian calendar still presents a few drawbacks. Not perpetual, the year does not always begin on the same day of the week. The months are of unequal length, and so are the quarters and half-years.

Introduced in France in 1792, the "Republican" year had twelve months of 30 days each, each month divided into three 10-day periods. This calendar was in use until January 1, 1806. In 1834, Marco Mastrofini, an Italian priest, came up with a revised "perpetual" Gregorian calendar.

The reform of the calendar is still being examined by the United Nations. The proposal provides for an annual cycle of

1

twelve months; the first month of each quarter would have 31 days and the others 30. To obtain the 365 or 366 days, one or two "dateless" days would be inserted, so the year and each quarter would always begin on a Sunday. The second month of each quarter, i.e. February, May, August and November, would begin on a Wednesday, and the four other months on a Friday. Each quarter would have ninety one days, each half-year 182, while each month would have 26 working-days, religious or national holidays notwithstanding.

The world might then finally have its perpetual calendar…

CALENDAR MOVEMENT and PERPETUAL CALENDAR

A calendar watch, or *quantième simple*, indicates not only the date, but also the day of the week, the month and sometimes the moonphase. This information is displayed by way of sub-dials, windows, and sometimes both combined. While quartz watches can be programmed to self-adjust to the different lengths of months, mechanical timepieces need to be fitted with a highly complicated mechanism to accomplish this feat. Thus, the *quantième perpétuel* and perpetual calendar are among the most appreciated watchmaking executions and refined complications.

2

1. The Marine P "Perpétuel" by Alain Silberstein. An automatic movement with a perpetual calendar. The days in red on the date circle are skipped based on the differences in the length of the months, and because of leap years.

2. Breguet skeletonized model of its impressive Tourbillon Perpetual Calendar showing day, date, month and leap years. The small second-hand is mounted on the tourbillon shaft. The blued-steel serpentine hand indicates the date.

1. The perpetual "Equation of Time"
by Breguet. The calculation of the
equation of time can be read between 1
and 2 o'clock. This automatic movement
also activates a power reserve indicator
displayed between 10 and 11 and a
complete perpetual calendar showing the
day, date, month and leap years.

2. When the two lines intersect, the daily
value of the equation of time is zero.
The equation of time attains its greatest
positive value on February 12 and its
greatest negative value on November 3.

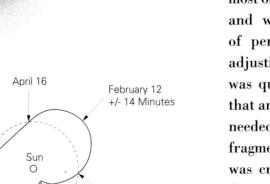

The *quantiéme perpétuel* – often associated
to the perpetual calendar – indicates the
ability of the movement to self adjust to the
specific number of days in each month: 28,
30 or 31. On the other hand, the
perpetual calendar is indeed a *quantième*
with the additional indication of the years
and leap-years. Completing one revolution
a year, the month-display mechanism
includes a small satellite wheel that takes
four full years to complete one rotation.
The perpetual calendar function enables
the watch to accurately display – with no
manual adjustments – the date, day,
month, and phases of the moon, even on
leap years. Years can be read on a sub-dial
displaying a four-year cycle with indication of
the bissextile year, or through an aperture.

THE EQUATION OF TIME

While it may be somewhat impossible for
most of us to simply apprehend the research
and work invested in the development
of perpetual calendar movements self-
adjusting for the next hundred years, it
was quite natural for Swiss watchmakers
that another system – even more complex –
needed to be invented to capture every
fragment of time not yet accounted for. So
was created the *Equation du Temps*, the
device indicating variations between mean
time and solar time.

As the Earth rotates around the Sun, its
elliptic course is quite irregular. Because of

its variable orbit, disparities occur in the duration of days. But if apparent solar time rules our planet, it does not govern our calendar which is based on an equal length of days throughout the year. Predictable planetary trajectories, enhanced by human design, have enabled mean solar time and real solar time to coincide four times a year. On April 16, June 14, September 1 and December 25, the equation will be 0. However, during the 361 remaining days of the year, reconciliation between real solar time and mean solar time will only be indicated on the equation of time, either positively from mid-December to late March and from June to September, or negatively in April and May and during the last four months of the year.

MOON PHASES

Calendar watches sometimes also show the phases of the moon: full moon, new moon and the quarters of the moon. These are usually displayed in illustrated form, with the image of the appropriate moon appearing through an aperture on the dial. Some moon phase designs are so refined that not only do they account for the lunar month, showing the twenty-nine and a half days with the various phases of the moon, but they also display the star systems and constellations at specific locations. One of the most famous examples is the Patek Philippe's Graves watch which accurately displays the starry skies of New York City…

FROM TOP

*Cartier's "Pasha" Perpetual Calendar.
A red dot indicates the leap-year cycle inside the month subdial, at 3 o'clock on the main dial.*

*Perpetual Calendar by Chopard.
The phases of the moon are shown at 6 o'clock, while the leap year is indicated by the roman numeral "4" in red on the leap year circle inside the month subdial located at 3 o'clock.*

FROM TOP

The "Replica" Perpetual Calendar Chronograph by Eberhard. The moon phase indicator is surrounded by the 12-hour counter of the chronograph, and the day and month are displayed on its 30-minute register.

The Breguet "Quantième." The moon phase indicator also displays the age of the moon on the half-circle graduated from 0 to 29 1/2, the length of a lunar month.

CHRONOGRAPH

The chronograph could be more properly called the *chronoscope*. But since this spectacular and useful complication is one of the last decade's most impressive successes of the watchmaking industry, we will leave pure terminology to rest. However, chronographs are still often mistaken with chronometers. Why? Probably because of the French. Indeed, the etymology of the word chronometer – instrument for measuring time – is shared, in French, with the word *chronométrage*, which means timing. In fact, when only a chronograph will record short time spans, the timepiece as a whole might as well be qualified as a chronometer if its movement was officially tested and received a certificate of accuracy.

A chronograph is a watch with hands showing the hours, minutes and seconds, combined with a mechanism controlling a chronograph-hand mounted in the center of the dial. By the operation of push-pieces, the chronograph-hand can be set in motion, stopped and returned to zero. The chronograph-hand will complete one revolution per minute, then a minute-register hand will record the number of revolutions, usually up to 30 minutes.

As the use of the chronograph increased with the progress of aeronotics and sports timing, some practical, hence technical,

CLOCKWISE FROM TOP LEFT

Chopard's "Mille Miglia" 1990 chronograph "rattrapante" and the 1993 tachometer chronograph wristwatch.

Cartier's "Pasha Chronoflex" with its galvanic dial and perpetual calendar accurate until the year 2100.

Breguet's "Type XX Aéronavale" chronograph with fly-back function.

Bvlgari's 18K yellow gold "Chronograph" is water resistant and has a quartz movement with a mechanical sweep second hand.

adjustments needed to be made. In response came the chronograph with fly-back function. The device allows the wearer to start the chronograph-hand, return it to zero and immediately restart it, thus skipping the two extra-steps of stopping and resetting the chronograph.

The "Rolls-Royce" of all chronographs, the split-seconds chronograph, or *rattrapante*, has two push-pieces and a "split" second-hand superimposed to the regular center second-hand. Used for timing several coincident events, both hands start simultaneously. At the end of the first span, the split-seconds hand is stopped, and the duration of the first event can be read on the dial; the split-seconds hand is then made to overtake the first hand, and continues to move with it. At the end of the second span, the split-seconds hand is stopped again, and the duration is read on the dial, and so on.

After the last timing, both hands can be stopped and returned to zero. One of the push-pieces controls the split-seconds hand alone, while the other controls both hands.

MINUTE REPEATER

The minute repeater is a complication that allows watches to tell time audibly, making it unnecessary to look at the dial.

A complex movement strikes the hours, quarter-hours and minutes on demand. In most cases, each strike has its own distinctive sound and frequency.

An advanced miniaturized adaptation of the clock mechanism, the minute repeater could be qualified as "the invention from the dark." In fact, before the introduction of the luminous paint and tritium-treated tips of the hands, it was impossible to tell time in the dark. Minute repeaters were manufactured to first respond to the needs of night travelers. From pure practicality to "Oeuvre d'Art," the minute repeater is considered today as one of the pinnacles of watchmaking.

Minute repeaters require a highly complex mechanical memory and the allied talents of a watchmaker, a metallurgist and a musician... Hammers and gongs will be designed and hand-adjusted to strike at least two contrasted tones, distinguishing the hours from the quarters and minutes.

At the push of a button, various types of repeaters will be heard: the hour strike, with one blow on the hour; the quarter repeater, sounding a low note for the hour and a "ting-tang" for each quarter; the five-minute repeater, striking the hours, quarters and five-minute periods after the quarters; and the minute repeater, striking the hours, quarters and minutes.

1 & 2 - Bvlgari's Répétition Minutes. Its intricate mechanism can be admired through the transparent back of the "Anfiteatro" platinum case. Note the two hammers on the lower left, engraved with an "H" for the hours and an "M" for the minutes.

3 - This classic minute repeater replicates one of Vacheron Constantin's design from the late 1930's. It contains an amazingly thin hand-wound movement measuring 3.30 mm. With a 48-hour power reserve, it strikes the hours, quarters and minutes at the press of a finger. Each of the 200 limited editions has a certificate of authenticity.

Time in a Thousand Pieces

The ultimate in melodious mechanisms is the *Grande Sonnerie*. Automatically striking the hours and quarters, the *Grande Sonnerie* will repeat the music of each of the tunes at the touch of a button.

"GRANDE COMPLICATION"

The *Grande Complication* is the supreme masterpiece, combining minute repeater, chronograph and perpetual calendar mechanisms. However, today's watchmakers have taken the extreme to even further limits with unique pieces also including a tourbillon and a split-seconds chronograph.

Among the most acclaimed timepieces is International Watch Company's "Grande Complication." Presented in 1990, the wristwatch required seven years in the making, including 50,000 hours of research to conceive its prototype and the synchronized interactions of its 659 mechanical parts housed in a 7.9 mm platinum case. Its chronograph records time spans up to 12 hours, and its perpetual calendar mechanism is set to accurately read the date for the next 120 years. With every part designed and manufactured at IWC, this masterpiece benefits from both the age-old discipline of master watchmakers and the advent of futuristic Computer Assisted Design. The "Coup de Maître" came three years later with "Il Destriero Scafusia." Limited to 125 pieces, this Grande Complication also houses a tourbillon and a split-seconds chronograph.

ABOVE

The "Grande Complication" by IWC.
This masterpiece, unveiled at the 1990 Basle Fair, took 7 years to build-including 50,000 hours of Research and Development- from the start of the project in 1983 to the first completed model on the 9th of April 1990, at 9:04 PM to be exact (a first functioning prototype was achieved in December of 1988). IWC took patents for twelve innovations on this watch. Among the most amazing of its 17 functions: a perpetual moon phase display accurate to 1 (one) day in 122 years (meaning a difference of 0.00066 day between two lull moons); a calendar -perpetual, of course- absolutely accurate until February 28 2100, displaying the date, day of the week, month, year, decade, and also century. The chronograph is accurate to 1/8th of a second. The 11 mm automatic movement can run for 48 hours fully wound and holds 65 jewels for the smooth running of its moving parts. Its balance is calibrated for 28,800 vibrations per hour. The hour, quarter-hour and minute repeater, with 720 striking combinations, rings a B flat for the hours and an E flat for the minutes. And it all fits in 178 grams of wristwatch.

OPPOSITE PAGE

The "Calibre 89" by Patek Philippe.
With its 33 complications, "Calibre 89" is a product of a "blue blood" lineage of technical masterpieces and the most complicated portable watch of all times. It took 9 full years to complete.The case, roughly 3.1/2 inches wide and 1.3/5 inches thick, weighs less than 3 pounds. It combines a "Grande Sonnerie" with 4 gongs striking the hours, quarters, five minutes and minutes, a chronograph "Rattrapante," a second time zone indicator, a perpetual calendar and moon phases. Its stars chart, coupled with the times of sunrise and sunset, rotates and accurately describes the skies as seen every night in Geneva only. It is, however, adjustable for any other place in the world. Patek Philippe can even install the appropriate gearing and stars chart for the Southern hemisphere. This mind-bogglingly intricate assembly of 2 dials, 8 disks, 24 hands, 68 springs, 129 rubies, 184 wheels, 332 screws, 429 mechanical components, etc., making a grand total of 1,728 parts, will even give you the date of Easter until the year 2017.
Four examples of the "Calibre 89" will ever be made, numbered 844 000 to 844 003, each in one shade of gold - yellow, rose - white and one in platinum.

1. The "Star Wheel"
by Audemars Piguet.
A marriage of poetry and invention,
the Star Wheel has the basic
design of an "aperture watch."
This automatic watch displays
the hour by means of three
sapphire discs, each of which
displays four of the twelve
hours. The watch has a
concentric circular aperture
graduated into minutes. The
secret of the Star Wheel is
simple: the three sapphire discs
are attached to a central wheel
which makes a complete
revolution every three hours.
Each disc, with an eight-point
star in the center, completes 1/8
of a revolution every half-hour.

2. The Jumping Hour in platinum
by Vacheron Constantin.
Under the silvered, engine-turned
dial, hour figures are inscribed on a
disc and "jumps every hour on the
hour" by one twelfth of a complete
rotation and are displayed in an
aperture at 12 o'clock. A raised
triangle, hand-tipped with onyx,
sweeps around the dial to show
the minutes on the rim of the dial.

3. The John Shaeffer Jumping Hour
with minute repeater by Audemars
Piguet. In 18K rose gold, this time
piece has a hand-wound movement
which activates the two white
enamel disks displaying the hours
at 12 and the minutes at 6.

POWER RESERVE

The power reserve, or *réserve de marche*, is
a feature increasingly found on mechanical
timepieces. The power reserve is actually
quite useful as it indicates how many hours
the watch would run if left untouched.

This surplus of power or additional running
time is calculated in excess of the normal
time between two consecutive windings: 24
hours for most movements, 7 days for those
requiring winding on a weekly basis, etc.

Although not necessarily displayed on the
dial, the power reserve indicator is usually
shown by a single hand running over a half-
moon shaped sub-dial, engraved with a scale
numbered either from 1 to 36 hours or from
1 to 48 hours, depending on the type of
movement.

JUMPING HOUR

The jumping hour, or *heure sautante*, is an
aesthetically breathtaking feature, which
has been only achieved by a few. It displays
the hour numeral through a window, also
called aperture or *guichet*, carved in the
dial.

Its sophisticated and curious nature makes
it a desirable object for collectors. The advent
of quartz movements and digital displays
marked the quasi-extinction of many of these
refined mechanical models of the Thirties.

LEFT TO RIGHT

Breguet's 18K yellow gold Tourbillon. Its hand-wound movement is engraved by hand. The triple-arrow of the small second-hand is mounted on and driven by the tourbillon shaft. Making three 120° angles, the three arrows run clockwise along the 20 seconds semi-circled dial fitted on the upper part of the tourbillon carriage.

Vacheron Constantin's platinum Tourbillon features a movement with twin series-coupled barrels, with its regulating unit, escapement and balance wheel mounted in a tourbillon carriage. The silvered "guilloché" dial displays three roman numerals and six applied gold markers with a power reserve indicator at 12.

Bvlgari's Tourbillon. The timepiece is enclosed in the elegant 18K yellow gold "Anfiteatro" case with champagne dial and applied gold markers. The rotation of the Tourbillon balance wheel is visible through an aperture on the dial.

Lately however, the jumping hour watch has seen a rebirth and many models are becoming collectible items sought-after by connoisseurs.

TOURBILLON

The *Tourbillon Régulateur* is regarded as one of genius watchmaker Abraham-Louis Breguet's greatest inventions. Designed in 1795 and patented in 1801, its object was to improve the precision of the watch movement by compensating for the effect of gravity on the balance wheel. First designed to address inaccuracies in the timekeeping of old pocket watches carried vertically, its principle was to create a device enclosing the entire balance mechanism. Then, the escapement and balance would be housed in a cage, also called carriage, mounted on a pivot and rotating on itself with absolute regularity, usually once every minute. This action causes the balance wheel and escapement to successively assume every vertical position. The balance rate is different if the heavier part of the assembly is either up or down. By rotating on itself inside the cage, the resulting rate errors cancel each other instead of accumulating.

Explaining his new invention in a letter to his son, Breguet presented the tourbillon as follows: "By distributing the resistances to different parts of the balance wheel and

ABOVE

A Patek Philippe Tourbillon regulator.

OPPOSITE PAGE

The skeleton minute repeater from Vacheron Constantin's "Les Complications" Collection has a hand-wound mechanical movement with repeating strike of the hours, quarter-hours and minutes. Its extra-thin movement is entirely decorated by hand and housed in a 18K pink gold case.

to the holes in which they turn and pivot..., I have been able to eliminate the anomalies created by the different positions of the center of gravity and the movement of the balance wheel."

Because of their exceptional beauty, most tourbillons are made visible, either through an aperture, a transparent case back, or as part of a skeletonized movement. To make sure that the tourbillon runs flawlessly, the cage must be perfectly concentric and all its components balanced. Very few firms have been able to successfully manufacture the tourbillon, contributing to its exclusiveness.

Tourbillons are generally located at 6 o'clock on the dial. However, modern master-watchmakers have pushed once again the limits of execution and tourbillon cages can now also be admired at 12 o'clock on Blancpain's Tourbillon and its remarkable skeleton version; centered, with Omega's Central Tourbillon; or, at 11 o'clock with the 1986 Audemars Piguet self-winding tourbillon. This extraordinary timepiece, the thinnest and the smallest of its kind, not only displays the tourbillon cage, but also reveals the pendulum oscillating weight for its self-winding mechanism through an aperture at 6 o'clock.

The location and decoration of the tourbillon cage are two major aesthetical issues for the horologist. Timepieces, such as Girard Perregaux's Tourbillon

under Three Gold Bridges, or *Tourbillon sous Trois Ponts d'Or*, or Jaeger-LeCoultre's Reverso Tourbillon, are breathtakingly intricate and beautiful.

The real thrill though is to actually combine the tourbillon with complications. Rare are those who have attempted the challenge, but how beautiful the outcome. Among them are the Breguet Tourbillon Perpetual Calendar, Corum's Tourbillon Minute Repeater, and Alain Silberstein's latest creation, the Tourbillon Chronograph.

The tourbillon regulator should also not be mistaken with the *Carrousel*. This less expensive system was devised by Bahne Bonnicksen, a Danish watchmaker residing in London. Bulkier, all its escapement parts were linear and rotated only once every fifty two and a half minutes. Temporarily used in the United States, the device was quite inferior in quality and performance. This attempt forced the watch industry to define and regulate the specifications of the tourbillon regulator to become exclusive to the most select watchmaking productions.

This mechanical architecture blossoms into a work of art. Swiss master watchmakers have always kept in mind the aesthetic value of a wheel or a balance mechanism, all these tiny little parts hidden deep in the heart of a timepiece. That is what places them way above mere watch manufacturers. They are the "Artists of Time."

LA MERV

Montre unique

AMI LECOULTRE-F

LE BRASSUS, VA

J.SPRENGER BIENNE

Montre 20 lignes à grande sonnerie, sonnant les heures et les quarts automatique
Chronographe avec compteur des minutes et rattrapante, ces mécanismes permettant de
teuse. Quantième perpétuel, indiquant les jours de la semaine, le quantième du mois, les p
Aiguille indicatrice du développement du ressort. Mécanisme isolateur du sautoir des min

LLEUSE

a-compliquée

JET, CONSTRUCTEUR

DE JOUX (SUISSE)

A VENDRE
Prix 20,000 Francs

CLICHÉ J.SPRENGER.

rmettant de répéter à volonté les heures, quarts et minutes. Avertisseur-réveil-matin
simultanément plusieurs observations. Double tour d'heures et aiguille de seconde trot-
unaires et l'année bissextile. Remontoir au pendant à triple effet et mise-à-l'heure double.
ystème Ami Lecoultre-Piguet. Echappement à ancre Balancier compensé.

Alain Silberstein is one of very few prestigious watchmakers to have become successful without a family tree of horologists behind him. In fact it was not until the eighties that this Parisian interior architect and industrial designer was initiated into the business. He broke his old LIP watch and was shopping for a new one. Unable to find the timepiece that would suit his modern style, he set about creating his own. After three years of dedicated technical research and design innovations, his first creation received an impressive response from his circle of acquaintances. Encouraged by this genuine and

Despite the relatively recent launch of the brand in the United States, the craze for Silberstein's creations now bridges the Atlantic to bring in over one-fifth of his annual world sales. His new concepts in watchmaking were like a breath of fresh air for an industry built upon traditional design. Silberstein's background in architecture gives his watches a unique look, quite different from the "Old School." His work embodies innovative architectural elements, venturing away from designs rooted in tradition. Avant-garde, contemporary, stylish and, above all, fun, Alain Silberstein's watches are

Alain Silberstein

unanimous enthusiasm, Silberstein took a few of his watches to display in a small booth tucked away in the back of the 1987 Basle International Watchmaking Fair. The overwhelming response came rather unexpectedly. He immediately garnered his first influential clients, mostly from Japan and Italy. Silberstein's watches rapidly gained success and popularity. Almost two thousand watches from six exclusive and limited edition lines were soon produced and sold in Germany, the United States, Japan, Italy, Great Britain and even Switzerland.

"unique objects viewed with a new eye... that capture the quintessence of Time." His creative vitality gained him respect and acceptance in the exclusive gentlemen's bastion of prestigious Swiss watchmakers. His entire production is manufactured in Besançon, the French hub of watchmaking, where he has nearby access to both French and Swiss watch centers. In a custom-built workshop on the banks of the river Doubs, his team of ten, including six professional watchmakers, develop each of his timepieces.

Alain Silberstein

ARCHITECTE HORLOGER

RIGHT

Alain Silberstein, architect and magician in the tourbillon of Time. "L' escamoteur à quatre temps."

PREVIOUS PAGE

To fittingly celebrate the 10th anniversary of his brand name in 1997, Alain Silberstein has created an exceptional watch combining his two watchmaking passions: the tourbillon and the chronograph. Only 10 watches will be made: each piece is unique with special case and dial finish.

LEFT

The HEBDO 2, with displays of the date, week and power reserve. An architectural back-ground and the Bauhaus artistic influence give Alain Silberstein's watches their unique look.

"Le vrai bonheur est d'avoir sa passion pour métier" – true happiness is making your passion your profession – is the philosophy of this Watch Architect. In Silberstein's mind, aesthetics and function are one and indivisible. Excellence is to be reached in every detail of his timepieces.

The movements – ETA, Lemania, Frédéric Piguet and Valjoux – which he carefully selected for his "Krono" and "Marine" lines have all received the prestigious "Three Star" stamp from the French CÉTÉHOR and certifi-cation of the Swiss C.O.S.C. These two organizations are responsible for qualifying movements as precision chronometers through a series of stringent tests.

When it comes to aesthetics, Silberstein's watches are exceptionally refined and different. In a survey run in 1995 by the select Italian watch-making magazine *L'Orologio*, Alain Silberstein Creations gained third place in the "Most Innovative" category. "Making watches is like being the conductor of an orchestra. The conductor creates and formulates the idea, but relies on all the parts of the orchestra to execute a perfect final symphony," states the young watch-maker-director.

MARINE P "PERPÉTUEL"

Limited to only a 100 pieces, the MARINE P is the second generation of Silberstein's "Perpétuel Marine." This automatic perpetual calendar is programmed to move from the 30th day of the month to the next 1st day, from February 28th to March 1st, and from February 29th to March 1st for leap years. To insure a more reader-friendly dial, months and years are positioned on a small dial on the transparent back of the watch. Distinctive of the "Marine" line, its movement is a chronometer certified by the C.O.S.C. and the time-piece is water resistant to 660 feet.

Disciplined in architecture and striving to relate form and function, his designs are conceived through the creative manipulation of three-dimensional space. Silberstein's inspiration comes from Modern Art movements. Klee, Malevich, the geometric works of the Cubists, and the De Stijl – a Dutch art movement – color rules of pure red, yellow and blue, and of "non-colors" black and white, are among the influences and styles incorporated into the design of his timepieces. Push buttons are color-coded according to their functions. The hour-hand is triangular and the second-hand a squiggly line. This clarifies the function of each watch part, clearly marked with colored enamels or luminous tritium-treated hands and indexes.

MARINE K

The MARINE K is the "ultra-sports" version of the famous KRONO watch. Adding to its chronographic functions, its Valjoux 7750 automatic movement also carries the date and a power reserve indicator located at 6 o'clock. Water resistant to 660 feet, its stainless steel case is topped with an anti-glare sapphire crystal. The MARINE K is also a limited edition of only 100 examples.

MARINE R "RATTRAPANTE"

The ultimate, the MARINE R features an automatic chronograph with split-seconds hand, date and power reserve.

Silberstein's "Marine Rattrapante" is characterized by its two chronograph second-hands: the yellow serpentine hand records the actual time, while the second serpentine, in white and red, records the intermediate time. The chrono-minutes are displayed are 12, the chrono-hours at 9, and the date can be read on the counter at 3.

This striking timepiece is made of an extra-hard stainless steel especially treated with carbon. Only a 100 examples will be produced, with a choice of black or white dial.

MARINE G

G is for G.M.T. Limited to 500 editions for both women and men, the Marine G is an automatic sports watch with the date and a simultaneous indication of two time zones.

133

During the 1995 Basle Fair, Alain Silberstein presented his Skeleton Tourbillon. Inspired by Cubist sculptures, the unique feature of this mind-boggling masterpiece resides in the integration of a tourbillon escapement into a movement reduced to its purest skeletonized lines. Each of the 20 editions that will ever be made is unique: the finish of the sapphire case, the movement parts in titanium, and the tourbillon bridge, dial plate and hands are specific to each watch. To celebrate this technical prowess and its watchmaker's passion, the barrel bridge is engraved with Silberstein's own quote: "Le vrai bonheur est d'avoir sa passion pour métier"

Silberstein's incorporation of the fine arts into industrial design was a move influenced by the Bauhaus School, the experimental German movement uniting painters, sculptors and architects through industrial design towards the same mode of expression in the early 20's. To finish each piece and show the dedication that he puts into his work, Silberstein signs and numbers each of his timepieces, and places them individually into a signature red leather pouch, inside an ultra-modern fiberglass box. Additional buckle-straps in red or CVD black finish coated metal bracelets are also provided, along with the tool to change straps and buckles. Each detail and finishing touch to his pieces creates Silberstein's *décor*, or "body work." The contemporary exactitude of the design complements the extreme precision of the movement within.

All of Silberstein's watches contain mechanical movements, most of them with complicated mechanisms, built as much for function as they are for aesthetics. He has created the most innovative designs to house traditional tourbillons, perpetual calendars, chronographs "rattrapante," and jumping hour, all displayed beneath a transparent glass case. The complexity of these movements has been continually updated and streamlined by the master watchmakers of all major movement manufacturers, making them a pinnacle of watchmaking ingenuity and achievement.

Silberstein's firsts in watchmaking include striking timekeepers such as the 1993 "Hébraïka," the first perpetual Hebraic calendar, and his latest first, the "Tourbillon Krono." This exceptional combination of a tourbillon and a chronograph was created to celebrate the tenth anniversary of the company. It is a limited edition of just ten pieces, each with a distinctive case and dial finish.

The "Tourbillon Krono" is Silberstein's icing on the cake of his "Krono" Collection started in 1987 with the Krono O, a hand-wound chronograph with complete calendar and moon phases. Since then, the "Krono" Collection has included the Kronoalarm, the Krono Bauhaus, whose design draws inspiration from the famous German art school of the 1920s, and the Krono Rattrapante, or split-seconds.

Its cousin, the "Kronomarine" series, offers a line tailored for the diver with models water-resistant to a depth of 660 feet. It features a carbone CVD black finish bracelet, front and back sapphire crystals, a polished stainless steel case, a uni-directional ratchet bezel, and enamel color-coded push-buttons corresponding to the functions of the watch, trademark of Silberstein's lines.

1. The movement of the KRONO A (top) with 37 jewels and the highly recognizable movement of the KRONO BAUHAUS (bottom).

2. The latest version of the KRONO CLASSIC displays a new assortment of colorful small hands indicating the date, day, 24 hours day-night, month, moon phases, and small seconds. Limited to 500 pieces and water resistant to 330 feet, this automatic three-counter chronograph with full calendar is driven by a certified C.O.S.C. chronometer which can be admired through a transparent caseback.

3. Limited to 100 pieces and water resistant to 330 feet, the automatic KRONO R, the ultimate split-seconds chronograph also features a power reserve indicator and a tachymetric scale.

4. The KRONO A, classic and automatic. This chronograph also features a date indicator located in the aperture at 6.

 *(page number)* 135

 *Alain Silberstein*

"Rolls Royce" of all chronographs, Silberstein's "Kronomarine Rattrapante," an automatic split-seconds chronograph, is one of the first diver's watches to include the split function in a mechanical diving watch.

The "Marine" Collection, which includes the "Kronomarine" series, comes in several versions with functions for all tastes: the Marine P, an automatic perpetual calendar; the Marine R, a new "Marine" version of the "Kronomarine Rattrapante" with an additional power reserve indicator; the Marine G, an automatic dual time; and the Marine K with power reserve, the "ultra-sport" version of Silberstein's famous Krono watch.

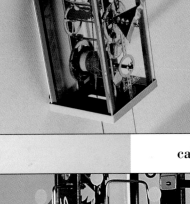

The "Perpétuel" is a series of perpetual calendar chronometers, developed with Danish master watchmaker Svend Andersen. The calendar is programmed to account for leap years and displays a reader-friendly dial with months and years on a small dial on the back of the watch. The "Perpétuel Marine" has a stainless steel case with a CVD black finish. Limited to a numbered series of 100, each watch comes with its own rotating leather gift box to keep the automatic movement wound up when not worn.

For centuries, standing clocks have regulated people's lives and then slowly disappeared from our homes. Alain Silberstein had always wanted to return the poetry of this "family totem" to his home, and like a kinetic sculptor, he created the KONTWAZ BAUHAUS.

Every year the Besançon work-shop makes a limited series of 100 clocks. The clock has the thematic shape and colors of the famous German art school of the 1920s. The KONTWAZ has a Comtoise movement built in Besançon. Chiming the half hours and hours, and then repeating the hours, the clock automatically stops from 10:30 pm to 8:00 am so as not to wake up its owner's home. The KONTWAZ BAUHAUS is also available in a mural version.

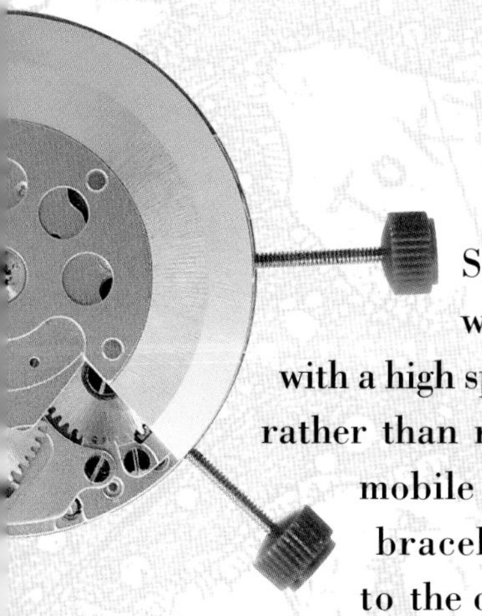

Silberstein's "Bolido" watches are streamlined, with a high speed profile, rectangular rather than round in form. With its mobile rollers, the Bolido bracelet is perfectly adapted to the curvature of the wrist.

Also striking is the "Bodoni" line. Its dial with raised numbers is a tribute to the great Italian painter Giambattista Bodoni (1740-1813), also famous for creating the magnificent typographical figures used on the off-center dial.

Another Silberstein's singular model is the "Cyclope," an automatic jumping hour. The face features only a sweep second-hand and an "eye" which gives the watch its name. The turning disk indicates the minutes along the edge of the dial. The hour is read inside the eye, on a rotating hour-register operated by a system of disks. The watch comes in steel, with either a black or white dial.

Each and every Silberstein's creation is a perpetual innovation in traditional watchmaking, a combination of the arts, from architectural principles to modernist painting and sculpture, combined inside a functional three-dimensional space of mechanical horology. Clearly the time was right to welcome the first Watch-Architect...

1

1. LE REVEIL is Alain Silberstein's automatic alarm with day, date and seconds. The alarm time is indicated by the white hand with the red arrow. Its movement is revealed above.

2. The KRONO BOLIDO is an addition to the already famous and collectible "Bolido" Collection. The automatic chronograph also features a date indicator at 6 o'clock. Streamlined with a high speed profile, its mobile rollers allow for the bracelet to be perfectly adjusted on one's wrist.

2

37

"Manufacture of quality complicated watches using the most modern methods of production…" was, and still is, the policy established by founders Jules Audemars and Edward Piguet. More than a century later, the company continues to honor the age-old tradition of craftsmanship: only 15,000 timepieces a year are assembled by hand, individually numbered and signed by the artisans of the manufacture in Le Brassus. The tradition began at the beginning of the 16th century when the ancestors of founder Jules Audemars moved to an isolated farmhouse in La Vallée de Joux. When watchmaking first made its

Audemars Piguet

appearance in the Valley in the mid-18th century, the family turned to it to supplement their income during the long winters. Born in 1851, Jules Audemars' early memories involved watching his father at the workbench, fabricating steel parts and assembling mechanisms for complicated pocket watches. Upon finishing primary school, Jules was sent to be further educated by the region's great horologists. His apprenticeship completed in 1873, he fine-tuned his craft working as a finisher, putting the ultimate touches on escapements of chronographs, calendar watches and repeaters.

Refusing to settle outside his native valley, newlywed Audemars decided to build his own workshop in his parents' farmhouse. Soon renowned throughout Switzerland for his creative high-quality work and flooded with more orders than his modest operation could fulfill, Audemars hired more watchmakers. Among them was Edward-Auguste Piguet. Piguet's family was one of the oldest in the Vallée de Joux. Like the Audemars, they farmed during summer months, but Edward's father, Charles-Auguste Piguet, was already known for opening a large, industrial-scale workshop in 1790 in Le Bas-du-Chenit. The production facility was the first of its kind in the region. When Edward completed his apprenticeship as a finisher and went on to work in Le Brassus, one of his customers was Jules Audemars. The two young men passionately discussed making more sophisticated and complicated watches. They had known each other since 1875, but it was only six years later that they decided to quit working as suppliers to establish their own manufactory. On the 17th day of December 1881, the partnership was made official by a ten-year contract, marking the birth of Audemars Piguet.

Audemars Piguet

TOP

The Audemars Piguet manufacture in Le Brassus, Vallée de Joux.

BELOW

Two talented master watchmakers: Jules-Louis Audemars (1851-1918) on the left and Edward-Auguste Piguet (1853 - 1919) on the right, joined forces in 1875 to found "Audemars Piguet & Cie."

BELOW

The "Grande Complication Savonette." One of many masterpieces that contributed to establish Audemars Piguet's name on the international scene. Audemars Piguet's first "Grande Complication" was presented at the Paris World Fair in 1889. Its movement, with over 400 components, drives a perpetual calendar displaying the date, month, moon phases and leap years, combined with a split-second chronograph and a minute repeater mechanism striking the hours, quarters and minutes at command.

CENTER

The "Automatic Triple Complication" carries Audemars Piguet's 2280 QP caliber, an automatic movement made of 650 components.

PREVIOUS PAGE

The "Royal Oak Offshore." Water-resistant down to a 100 meters, its design is sporty and rugged. Its movement is automatic, driving a date indicator hand on the outside ring and a small second-hand on a subdial at 6 o'clock.

Under the agreement, Jules Audemars was named technical director and Edward Piguet commercial and financial director. Today the spirit of this union lives on with their descendants, who since its creation continue to sit on the company's board of directors. The strength of family tradition promotes the quality of the company's products and contributes to the prestige of Audemars Piguet watches.

Since its inception, the company has been a pioneer in high-performance watch movements, maintaining its reputation for having distinctive designs and using high-grade materials and ultra-flat movements. On the year of its creation, Audemars Piguet manufactured its first "Grande Complication," with minute repeater, perpetual calendar with moon-phases, minute counter, and a split-second chronograph. The company stood out not only for its technical prowess, but also for the originality of its designs. In 1911, Audemars Piguet created one of the first complicated jeweled wristwatches. Beautifully set with diamonds, the model had a small ten-line caliber with a minute repeater and a distinctive centre second - hand. In the fall of 1918, at the age of 67

Jules Audemars died, followed a few months later by his partner. Still, the company's achievements would continue to read like the Guiness Book of Records with an incredible number of world firsts: in 1925 the world's thinnest pocket watch, only 1.32 mm; in 1946 the world's thinnest wristwatch with a 1.64 mm movement; and in 1967, a new record with the thinnest automatic movement, 2.45 mm with a 21K gold rotor... In the 1970s, Audemars Piguet was to create the timepiece that would become the standard bearer of its century-old watchmaking tradition: a new icon was born with the creation of the Royal Oak. Associated with royalty since 1651, when King Charles II of England found refuge from his pursuers in the hollow of an ancient oak, the name Oak was adopted by the Royal Navy for a series of vessels which sailed at the height of imperial glory. This royal and naval heritage inspired the porthole-shape of Audemars Piguet's Royal Oak design: octagonal with eight hexagonal screws. Launched in 1972, the Royal Oak epitomized the perfect balance between virile power and elegance.

This highly successful model would later be reissued in several editions: the Royal Oak Jubilé with an ultra-thin automatic movement, and in 1993, the striking Royal Oak Offshore. Designers opted there for an even more rugged case-thickness than that of the classic Royal Oak, with gaskets made of synthetic material to add impact resistance. A magnifying crystal ensures optimum visibility on the date, and fluorescent tritium-treated hands and markers brightly glow in the dark. The Royal Oak Offshore has an automatic movement with a 21K gold rotor, set in a satin-finished case, with a date indicator at three o'clock and a small second-hand. With each piece requiring nearly one year to produce,

ABOVE LEFT

The "Royal Oak Dual Time" in two-tones. A single automatic movement serves for both time zones, another first for Audemars Piguet. Two subdials indicate the date at 3 o'clock and the secondary time zone at 6. The 48-hour power reserve indicator is displayed between 8 and 11.

ABOVE RIGHT

The "Royal Oak Automatic Perpetual Calendar" in its skeletonized version, with its four subdials: months at 12 o'clock, date at 3, phases and age of the moon at 6, and days of the week at 9 o'clock.

LEFT

Two-tones "Royal Oak Automatic," in titanium and 18K yellow gold. To gold, Audemars Piguet adds Tantalum, a high density metal (16.6), very resistant to heat. First presented at the 1972 Basle Fair, the line now includes more than 20 models for ladies and men, including the "Offshore" diving watch and new jewelry variants.

CHRONOGRAPH
WITH AUTOMATIC PERPETUAL CALENDAR

This "Chrono Quantième" combines chronographic and perpetual calendar functions displayed on a striking black dial framed by the engraved bezel of a rose gold case. The 3 o'clock subdial shows the phases of the moon. Other counters combine two indications each: at 12, the date and small seconds; at 6, the day and chronograph 12-hour counter; the chronograph 30-minute register and leap year at 9 o'clock. The tachymetric scale is located around the second-circle for the chronograph hand.

THE "STAR WHEEL"

The automatic Star Wheel allows one to read the hour by means of three sapphire discs, each displaying four of the twelve hours. The watch has a concentric circular aperture graduated in minutes. The secret of the Star Wheel is simple: the three sapphire discs are attached to a central wheel which makes a complete revolution every three hours. Each disc, with an eight-point star in the center, completes 1/8 of a revolution every half-hour. Available in platinum, yellow and rose gold, its case and face are finely decorated and "guilloché" by hand.

AUTOMATIC TOURBILLON II

This very sober platinum case in three parts with a brushed caseband holds an automatic movement with the tourbillon in a titanium frame visible at 6 o'clock. The hours and minutes are displayed on the offset dial with roman numerals by browned gold hands, while the small hands indicating the date and power reserve at 3 and 6 are in blued-steel. The black crocodile strap is attached to pear-shaped horns and fastened to the wrist with a platinum clasp. This model is also available in a skeletonized version with a gold case.

PERPETUAL CALENDAR SKELETON

The "Quantième Perpétuel Cambré Gravé" has an extra-flat hand-wound movement, with a power reserve of about 40 hours. It drives browned gold hour and minute hands on a part skeletonized, part finely engraved face with roman numerals on a sapphire glass plate. The date is displayed at 3, the phases and age of the moon at 6, the day of the week at 9, and the month at 12 o'clock. The 2805 perpetual calendar mechanism is only 1.55 mm thick, which puts the whole mechanism at 3.20 mm.

CALIBRE 2003

1946 saw the creation of the extra flat ML caliber, just 1.64 mm thick. To celebrate its 50th anniversary, the House unveiled a special limited edition of 300 watches: 150 in yellow gold, 100 in rose gold and 50 in grey gold. The difference with the original model is a transparent caseback.

the case's gleaming finish is achieved through four separate hand polishings, and acquires its shape after twenty precise assembling operations. The last delicate operation is to test the case water-resistance to 10 Atm. The powerful design of the Royal Oak lent itself to many interpretations, with the use of new materials and complicated features: automatic perpetual calendar, dual time and phases of the moon, in steel, yellow gold and two-tones.

Audemars Piguet's fame is not quite confined to the Royal Oak. In 1992, true to its remarkable history of technical innovations, the company presented its

"Triple Complication," highlight of its modern watchmaking history. It is one of the most complicated watches in the industry: in addition to twelve different functions, including display of the day, date, month and phases of the moon, its 600 parts – assembled by hand – activate a perpetual calendar allowing for self-adjusting leap years, a minute repeater which strikes on the minute, quarter-hour or hour as desired, and a split-second chronograph precise to 1/5 of a second with a separate 30-minute counter.

Housed in a case only 8.55 mm thick, the automatic movement with 52 jewels and a rotor made of 18K gold is entirely hand-made by the highly skilled Audemars Piguet's craftsmen. Only five are produced each year, and each one undergoes four months of setting and adjustment. The company offers a complete collection of complications, all set in contemporary designs: an automatic Tourbillon and its skeleton version, minute repeater with jumping hours, Grande Sonnerie, chronograph with automatic perpetual calendar, automatic dual time, and the unique Star Wheel. The secret of the Star Wheel is simple: three sapphire discs attached to a central wheel that makes a complete revolution every three hours. Each disc, with an eight-point star in the center, completes 1/8 of a revolution every half-hour, indicating the hours on an aperture graduated in minutes. It is the ultimate in watchmaking: authenticity, intelligence and aesthetic perfection.

Also striking for its originality are Audemars Piguet's "John Schaeffer" minute repeaters. Created in 1907 for a very rich American industrialist fascinated with the musical complication, the initial model was bearing letters to spell out his name on each index. One of the most sought-after of all the Manufacture's celebrated timepieces, the watch is able to

strike the hours, quarters and minutes, and when desired, hammers the time in two tones.

Recently, Audemars Piguet presented the "Millenary" line. Based on the concept of a "horizontal oval," both strikingly new and recognizably classic, the shape, neither cambered nor curved represents an entirely new departure from earlier Audemars Piguet collections. The case can accommodate even the most complex movement, with easy-to-read displays. Among the "Millenary" novel technical features, is an "inertia-block balance" preventing the disturbances due to internal phenomena such as bending or dampening, thereby enhancing reliability. The dial is original, accentuating the oval shape while maintaining a purity of line. The "Millenary" line comes in many variations, including steel, gold in shades of pink, grey or yellow, with polished bezel or brushed bevel. The "Millenary" also offers a broad range of technical models: the Chronograph,

ABOVE LEFT

The "Roberta" line is the Manufacture's latest creation, a line of exceptional ladies watches. Rounded in shape, but elongated at the bracelet, the model is designed for ladies of exceptional taste. All the diamonds used in the creation of the "Roberta" watches are of IF Top Wesselton quality.

ABOVE RIGHT

A touch of nostalgia with the "Carrée" with small seconds at 6 o'clock. Based on a 1944 design, this 18K yellow gold square wristwatch has an extra-thin hand-wound 22-jewel movement. Its dial, in a design similar to the original, displays applied gold Arabic numerals and browned gold "feuille" hands.

UP LEFT

A hand-wound movement, enclosed in a tonneau-shaped rose gold case, animates the "John Shaeffer" Jumping Hour with Minute Repeater. The hours "en sautant" jump in the aperture at 12 o'clock, while the minute-disk rotates smoothly at 6. The two-tone repeater is activated by pressing the push-piece on the left side of the case.

LEFT

The Minute Repeater "John Shaeffer Star Wheel." Based on the mechanism of the "Star Wheel," this minute repeater displays hours and minutes by way of rotating sapphire glass disks.

BOTTOM RIGHT

The "Millenary" Perpetual Calendar. This unusual oval-shaped automatic watch displays the day, date, month, leap-year, phases and age of the moon, and a week counter served by a golden arrow around the minute and hour circle.

ABOVE

The "Millenary" line.
The watch that will celebrate the arrival of the third millennium under the colors of Audemars Piguet has to be a truly exceptional watch. And so it is. This complete new collection includes all possible complications and takes design beyond every known frontier. Like creation itself, the Millenary is a paradox, taking the form of an oval with its horizontal, fascinatingly novel and instantly classical shape.

From left to right: the Day-Date with small seconds at 6, and the days on the edge of the dial, framed by a pink gold case; the Automatic in yellow gold; the Dual Time; the Chronograph with date calendar; the Pilot with black dial and tritium-treated hands and indexes; the Perpetual Calendar with phases and age of the moon; and, to the far right, the Day-Date in yellow gold with cabochon sapphire winding crown.

the Dual Time, an ultra-flat Automatic Perpetual Calendar, The Aviateur, with its striking black dial, the Day Date, and the Day Date Month "à guichet."

Audemars Piguet's early watchmaking and marketing genius also came noticed in the advance of ladies' wristwatches: smaller, thinner, increasingly accurate and complicated movements could finally be fitted in slimmer, thinner, more delicate cases. Designed "to capture the feminine universe, its moods, its sensitivity, its flights of fancy," Audemars Piguet's "Carnegie," "Opera," "Grande Dame," and "Roberta" lines testify to the company's long tradition of creating

exceptional watches for women. Watches and bracelets are varied so "ladies on all continents can look forward to the fulfillment of their wildest dreams." Audemars Piguet's "Carnegie" collection features a wristwatch designed for "ladies with an independent streak." Another famous millionaire inspired the "Carnegie" collection: Andrew Carnegie, whose lavish lifestyle was refined by a tasteful sobriety. Though he went on to be one of America's wealthiest industrialists, he never forgot his humble beginnings. Philanthropist in the scientific and cultural fields, he endowed trusts, charities, and over 3,000 libraries. In the 1940s, changes in fashion and contemporary design provided

fresh inspiration to Audemars Piguet's engineers, who began to work on a movement for a truly flat watch. By 1946, the ML calibre was developed. The movement had a nine line diameter, and a thickness of just 1.64 mm. Even by today's standards, the ML 1946 calibre is still considered a remarkable achievement. A tribute to Andrew Carnegie, the watch's barrel-shaped design is reminiscent of the 1920s, hinting at the "unknown promise of time's distant horizon." Dedicated to the woman of independent temperament, the new ladies' "Carnegie" collection is available with leather straps in many colors, as well as bracelets, in grey gold, or steel.

The case comes in grey or yellow gold, plain or set with diamonds.

Avant-gardist in watchmaking, Audemars Piguet was also a pioneer in marketing its timepieces. One of the first companies to expand its public exposure by sponsoring sporting events and fund-raisings, Audemars Piguet impacted and educated many. High-society crowds, anonymous collectors and generations of watch lovers have learned not just about the Manufacture in Le Brassus "striving for perfection" in its Art, but also about a unique family of artisans who give a taste of it in each of their creation.

LEFT

The new Audemars Piguet "Carnegie" collection features the wristwatch for ladies of an independent frame of mind. The line is inspired by the "self-made" Andrew Carnegie and his remarkable lifestyle, as reflected by the great man's legendary Skibo Castle estate in Scotland, a monument combining wealth of means with sobriety of character. The barrel-shaped design of this unique watch is at once an evocation of a memorable period of modern history, the 1920s, and of the future with its promise of the unknown. The "Carnegie" for ladies is available with leather straps in different colors, as well as cases and bracelets in yellow gold, grey gold or steel, plain or set with diamonds and precious gemstones.

LEFT

The "Grandes Dames" collection offers a variety of jewelry watches set with diamonds and superior quality precious stones. Each jewel-set watch comes with a certificate attesting to the purity, colors, weight and cut of the gemstones.

BELOW

A men's skeleton watch from the early fifties, with an engraved movement. The roman numerals are unusually displayed on the bezel. This model is one of the first skeleton watch ever.

Audemars Piguet

Since the time of the Middle Ages, the Baume family was a powerful force, a family of notable landowners in the Franche-Comté region. During the sixteenth century, Louis-Joseph Baume sensed the importance of the emerging watchmaking industry in Switzerland and set up a workshop in the heart of the Jura mountains. Later, his descendants established a factory and, in 1834, officially registered the Baume Frères Company in Bois. From that point on, the Baume family name established itself as one of the oldest, most prestigious line of watchmakers.

His brother, Victor Baume, ran the factory. In 1878, the company was renamed Baume & Co. The company received top honors at several of the World's Trade Fairs for their work in horology. Baume was also the triumphant winner of the competition organized by the Kew Observatory in 1893, earning the still-unrivaled rating of 91.9 out of 100 for a "keyless chronometer with tourbillon movement." This prize opened the doors to British international trade, and with it, members of high society and royalty from around the world became clients.

Baume & Mercier

When the Industrial Revolution made possible the arrival of the first chronographs, the Baume Frères proudly introduced some of the earliest models. One of the brothers invented a new escapement which allowed him to reduce the thickness of the watches by a considerable amount. In 1847, Pierre-Joseph Célestin Baume set out for Great Britain to develop a network of business contacts. Not only did he meet people in the industry, but he also opened a subsidiary watchmaking company, Baume Bros. in London, to import and distribute their exclusive models from Bois.

By the close of the 19th century, Baume & Co.'s business was rapidly expanding in the British colonies and the Far East. By streamlining production and honing their creative skills, the Baumes became trailblazers in international watch marketing. Between 1878 and 1889, the company was awarded six gold medals at the universal exhibitions held in Paris, Melbourne, Zurich, London, Chicago and Amsterdam. The twentieth century would bring upon new alliances and the most exciting business developments in its history.

BUREAU OFFICIEL DE L'ÉTAT
POUR LE CONTRÔLE FACULTATIF

DES MONTRES DE GENÈVE

DIPLÔME

En exécution de l'arrête du Conseil d'Etat du 11 Juillet 1913,

Le Département du Commerce et de l'Industrie de la

République et Canton de Genève delivre à

Messieur Baume & Mercier

In 1912, William Baume met Paul Tchereditchenko, the son of a czarist officer and head of the Geneva firm of watchmakers-jewelers. Tchereditchenko moved to Switzerland to be close to his trade and changed his name to Mercier.

Their personalities could not have been more different: Baume was reserved, a man of moderation, deeply attached to his family name and reputation; Mercier was dynamic and outgoing, a man of refined tastes and a lover of art. Many of his friends were artists, and his wife was related to neo-Impressionist Edouard Fer. However, the two men respected each other's talents, and the alliance proved to be fruitful. On November 26, 1918, the two men consolidating their business ties by creating Baume & Mercier in Geneva. Combining Baume's technical expertise and Mercier's design, the House rapidly gained notoriety.

In 1921, the company was awarded the Poinçon de Genève, the highest honor given to master watchmakers by the Republic and Canton of Geneva. The fledgling company was on its way to worldwide acclaim. The award was a glorious acknowledgment of the quality of the firm's work, and pushed the two men to higher creative levels.

1. *Two men, a single great destiny: Louis-Victor Baume (left) and Paul Mercier (right).*

PREVIOUS PAGE

The Baume & Mercier Linea collection offers this spectacular model with a gold dial, polished gold case and bracelet, set with 500 diamonds. Also available in white gold, the timepiece is water resistant to 99 feet and carries Baume & Mercier's emblem, the Phi symbol stamped on its gold crown.

Despite the international economic depression in the post-war years, Baume & Mercier continued its growth. Much of this expansion owes itself to the roaring 20's and the 30's. These were extraordinarily fertile times for the arts. During this prolific period, Baume & Mercier recreated the classic onion-shape watch in new shapes, to be round, square or rectangular. Pocket watches gave way to wristwatches and were set with gems to be worn as jewelry. Time progressed and Baume & Mercier's production of chronographs expanded in response to a growing world demand.

In 1964, the company introduced its first watch bearing the Phi symbol. Inspired by the Greek letter, Phi symbolizes many things – it represents the "Golden Number," a theory of proportion and balance, renamed the "divine proportion" by Leonardo da Vinci. The Phi symbol has since become the signature for the clasps and dials of all Baume & Mercier watches. It represents the brand's fundamental values–expertise, the highest standards of workmanship, attention to detail and a commitment to quality.

The 1960s also saw the formation of a "new look" for the new woman. The revival of Haute Couture fashion spurred women to "dress up" before they went out. Recognizing this trend, Baume & Mercier created lines of elegant watches to complement the new look. The "Marquise" model was created, featuring a case which was incorporated in a rigid silver, claspless bracelet. Baume & Mercier also made notable developments in the area of technology, including the creation of the planetary rotor. The device oscillated the movements of the wrist to "wind" the watch and activate the main spring. This led to the production of the world's flattest self-winding watch with day and date available. In 1971, one of the first tuning fork movements was created for the Tronosonic Collection. The company went on to receive the prestigious Golden Rose of Baden-Baden award for the aesthetics of the Galaxie, Mimosa and Stardust models in 1973. These watches were examples of Baume & Mercier's devotion to art. For enamel pocket watches, the house offered special order reproduction paintings of modern masters such as Morandi or Giorgio De Chirico.

2   **3**

149

Baume & Mercier

1

1. *Baume & Mercier enamel pocket watch*

2. *Baume & Mercier onion-shaped watch*

3. *Baume & Mercier "Marquise" watch with face integrated into the rigid bracelet which enclosed the wrist.*

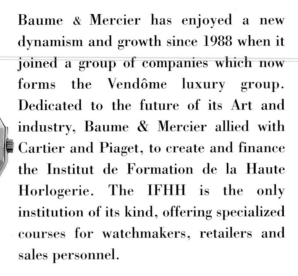

Baume & Mercier has enjoyed a new dynamism and growth since 1988 when it joined a group of companies which now forms the Vendôme luxury group. Dedicated to the future of its Art and industry, Baume & Mercier allied with Cartier and Piaget, to create and finance the Institut de Formation de la Haute Horlogerie. The IFHH is the only institution of its kind, offering specialized courses for watchmakers, retailers and sales personnel.

The factories where Baume & Mercier watches are assembled must meet strict quality controls, tested at each stage of production. Each timepiece takes a complete year to evolve from the initial sketch to presentation. Within a light-filled design studio, designers consider the aesthetic purpose of each technical advance. Electronic technology is used to produce extremely flat, elegant cases. The cases are accurate to a hundredth of a millimeter, each requiring fifteen die stamping and finishing operations. At the same time, research is continually being done on new materials.

This research allows the design team of Baume & Mercier to set trends, not follow them. And this is important to Baume & Mercier's international clientele who seek innovative designs that reflect their personal tastes. The company offers a comprehensive array of designs which are distributed each year in over 3,000 authorized retail jewelers in 75 countries worldwide. Functional sports watches and classic jewelry watches combine elegant taste and technical expertise. In Baume & Mercier, consumers have found a luxury Swiss watchmaker who believes in the quality of its timepieces while upholding the highest customer service standards.

Baume & Mercier's signature piece, the Riviera, is distinctive for its unique shape. In 1973, this timepiece was introduced, based upon a simple concept: "As a watch has 12 numbers, the Riviera will have 12 sides." So the model was bestowed with a twelve-sided bezel. More than 20 years later, this watch remains a best seller for combining elegance and sophistication with advanced technical features. Water resistant, the Riviera is available in a variety of styles for both men and women in stainless steel, stainless and 18K gold or all 18K gold, with the option of diamonds. Each features an alternating satin-finished and polished metal link bracelet to comfortably fit the wrist.

The most prestigious model of the Baume & Mercier collection is the Milleis. This limited edition watch highlights a century and a half of expertise and exceptional craftsmanship on which the company has built its reputation.

1. The Riviera in stainless steel with Arabic numerals and engraved dial.

2. Man's Riviera in stainless steel showing a white guilloché face with Roman numerals and date indicator at 6.

3. The ladies' Riviera model displays a striking wrist-hugging bracelet in stainless steel and 18K yellow gold.

4. The man's Riviera version in 18K yellow gold.

1

2

Every component of the Milleis watch must meet the highest standards in watchmaking tradition. It is equipped with accurate hand set mechanical and automatic movements designed exclusively for the knowledgeable watch connoisseur. The case, hands, markers and crowns of this watch are made of 18K yellow gold, making it the most prestigious men's watch in the complete line. For those who prefer a softer look, the model is also available in pink gold. Milleis is designed for the man with a passion for watchmaking tradition, the man who appreciates the unmistakable look of individuality and quality of this magnificent line.

The Malibu sports watch is designed for a more contemporary customer looking for a watch of character that combines technical performance and sheer elegance. It contains an automatic movement within an interesting style that includes an engraved bezel with Roman numerals.

The Malibu is sporty yet elegantly simple, without the "busy" extraneous features of many sports watches. The new Malibu chronograph model has been developed with flawless technical characteristics. The case houses a tachymetric scale, hour and minute counters as well as a date window. Its screw down back and lockable screw-in push pieces guarantee total water resistance up to 90 feet.

1. *The Milleis, in its men's version features an automatic movement, a mat white solar guilloché face with 18K yellow gold Dauphine hands and bar hour markers on a brown crocodile strap.*

2. *The Malibu Chronograph is ideal for the free-spirited adventurer. This timepiece houses an automatic movement with 40-hour power reserve. Its bezel is elegantly engraved with Roman numerals.*

1   **2**   **3**

1. *Hampton Dual Time Zone in stainless steel*

2. *Hampton with its curved polished stainless steel case and tobacco calf leather strap with deployment buckle in stainless steel.*

3. *Several feminine designs characterizes the Ilea Collection. The Ilea was created for the woman who prefers to wear her timepiece as jewelry. The watch is water resistant to 99 feet. Its crown is set with a synthetic cabochon sapphire.*

4. *Three stainless steel Hampton models: clock wise, ladies' model with strap, men's model with bracelet and tonneau-shaped model.*

4

The Hampton model reflects the brand's philosophy, balancing tradition and modernity with its retro charm and contemporary elegance. Launched in 1993, it has already obtained worldwide recognition. The curved, rectangular shape gives the stainless steel watch a distinctive, classic look. The tonneau shape is the perfect evolution of the original rectangular model adding softness to its geometrical balance. The Hampton offers a collection of both men's and women's watches in a variety of straps and dials, including a dual time zone. Available on a stainless steel bracelet each link is an extension of the unique case design. The stainless steel folding clasp on a leather strap is one of the model's distinguishing characteristics. Hampton affirms Baume & Mercier's position as a design leader in the sport-classic steel watch category. Elegant, unique and

strongly identifiable, the Hampton will enjoy longevity over the years.

Ilea is the name given to Baume & Mercier's extensive jewelry collection. Gleaming with polished gold or sparkling with diamonds, every detail of an Ilea watch is designed to make a woman feel radiant. Whether she chooses her Ilea timepiece with her heart or mind, she can be reassured that each watch is adorned with highly polished gold and the highest quality diamonds. Uniquely crafted, the Ilea demonstrates the perfect integration between the bracelet and the watch case; each complementary of the other. Befitting of the most luxurious jewelry watches, a synthetic cabochon sapphire graces the winding crown.

The Baume & Mercier Linea Collection is the most prestigious of all jewelry bracelets, a fashionable and contemporary

model made for women. Its styling and design reflect soft femininity with sculpted links that give the appearance of a bracelet with a watch. Each gold link of the bracelet is meticulously polished for a perfect glow. Its look appeals to the woman who wants to wear a watch as jewelry, all day, every day. The line offers a series made from stainless steel to 18K gold and diamond to suit individual lifestyles and personal preferences. The creative designed bezel is engraved with distinctive Arabic numerals. Master craftsmen have adorned the dial, case and bracelet of the most luxurious Baume & Mercier Linea with 500 brilliant diamonds, totaling 4.8 carats. This stunning piece is produced in a very limited series for the ladies' dress watch category, an area in which Baume & Mercier is know for its excellence.

Baume & Mercier offers a comprehensive selection of styles for all tastes, all possessing the uncompromising quality of design and precision technical features that have established Baume & Mercier as a leader in the watchmaking industry. Today, the firm uses its unique position in the market place to combine the finest in quality craftsmanship and unparalleled customer service with a contemporary design vision that continues to appeal to an ever expanding international clientele.

As the brand's inherent value remains timeless, each Baume & Mercier owner can maintain confidence in knowing their timepiece will provide them with great joy today and tomorrow for the generations to come.

FROM LEFT TO RIGHT

Baume & Mercier's Linea in stainless steel, with white dial and Arabic numerals engraved on the bezel; the two-tone version enhanced by a blue dial; the 18K yellow gold, with mother-of-pearl dial and Arabic numerals engraved on the bezel; the 18K yellow gold with diamond bezel; and the 18K gold dial and polished case, set with 500 diamonds throughout the watch.

BOTTOM

Baume & Mercier's Petra. An elegant 18K gold, diamond-set bracelet watch. Twelve diamonds mark the hours on a mother-of-pearl dial.

"To carry a fine Breguet watch is to feel that you have the brains of a genius in your pocket." Testifying to these words by Sir David L. Salomons in 1921, original order books, company registers and workshop notes detail much of Abraham-Louis Breguet's genius. Considered by many as the father of watchmaking, Breguet is one of the greatest horologists of all times. The company's ledgers bear witness to the most exclusive clientele: Marie-Antoinette, Napoléon Bonaparte, the Prince of Wales, the French Royal Navy, King Farouk of Egypt, the Sultan of the Ottoman Empire, the Duke of Windsor,

Upon completing exceptionally thorough horological studies and a complete mathematics curriculum at the Collège Mazarin under Abbé Marie, Breguet decided to settle in the French capital. Marie soon introduced him to the Royal Court where he found his first patrons. In 1775, Breguet set up shop at No.39 of Quai de l'Horloge, renting the fourth floor of a building owned by the Duchess of Polignac. The young man was soon inducted into Paris' social scene. His impressive gifts and growing reputation earned him the esteem of many crowned heads and leading figures of his epoch, including Marie-

Alexander Dumas and Sir Winston Churchill, just to name a few. Spanning from royalty throughout Europe to aeronautical and maritime forces, the diversity of the company's many clients is a testament to Breguet's multi-disciplinary approach to watchmaking. Born in 1747 in Neuchâtel, Abraham-Louis Breguet was barely eleven years old when his father passed away. The remarriage of his mother to Joseph Tattet marked the beginning of Breguet's watchmaking career. In 1762, Tattet took the young boy to Paris to serve apprenticeship for a reputed watchmaker established in Versailles.

Antoinette, Queen of France, who made Breguet's watches fashionable in the Versailles circles. For the Queen, Breguet created the famous bejeweled timepiece bearing her name. Commissioned as a gift by an officer of her guard, the timepiece was not completed until after her death. Today, the "Marie Antoinette" is considered one of the most complicated horological masterpieces in the world. Escaping destruction during the French Revolution, the watch passed through many hands before Sir David Salomons donated it to a museum in Israel. Sadly, the masterpiece got stolen from the museum and was never recovered.

ABOVE

Breguet designed the "Marie Antoinette" for the Queen of France whose name it bears.

RIGHT

Pocket watch in 18K yellow gold. Its hand-wound movement drives a perpetual calendar showing the day, date, month and leap-years, as well as the phases and the age of the moon. Its "Grande Sonnerie" chimes the hours, quarter hours and minutes with three different gongs. This piece is unique.

BELOW

The plate of the "Anno 1794." Breguet started working on this perpetual watch with moon phases and power reserve indicator on April 4, 1787 and sold it to Count Journiac St. Méard in 1794.

PREVIOUS PAGE

An utterly exceptional composition combining the technical achievement of minute repeater watches with the magnificence of precious stones.

Forced to flee during the French Revolution's most tragic hours, Breguet sought refuge back in Switzerland in 1793. Yet his forced exile turned out to be highly productive and Breguet secured new alliances with some of Geneva and La Vallée de Joux's best craftsmen. In 1795, Breguet returned to Paris to find his workshop partially destroyed. Ironically, the wars in Europe and the emergence of a post-revolution new elite served only to strengthen Breguet's business. With the assistance of his son Antoine-Louis, Breguet rebuilt his atelier and began designing his own "calibres" for simple and repeater watches. His production increased dramatically to reach the farthest corners of Europe. A new network of agents started representing the firm from London to Madrid, Constantinople and Moscow, where Leon Tolstoï even used Breguet's name as a synonym for "chronometer." During this prolific period, the firm's sales journals read like the "Who's Who" of Russian nobility. In 1810, King Louis XVII of France appointed Breguet as Watchmaker to the Royal French Navy. The result was the "Breguet Marine," an exceptionally accurate chronometer. Offsprings of this model still exist in the company's current lines and remain an example of watchmaking intelligence and precision. Breguet linked his name to some of the most pivotal inventions, technical achievements and aesthetic standards.

His creations influenced many of his contemporaries who adopted his styles during the Empire period.

Towards the end of his life, Breguet received many honors in recognition of his achievements and contributions to his Art. Elected to the *Académie Royale des Sciences* in 1816, he was also named *Chevalier de la Légion d'Honneur*, and a member of the French Bureau of Longitudes. By then, Abraham-Louis Breguet had already made his mark on watchmaking history by elaborating new mechanisms and aesthetic principles. To name a few, in less than twenty years, Breguet had perfected the basic development of the "perpétuelle," or self-winding watch; created the first escapement to work without oil; designed the earliest shock absorber for the timepiece; developed the perpetual date calendar, and in 1795 invented the complex "Tourbillon," the ultimate mechanism which eliminates the fluctuation of a watch's performance due to the effects of gravity. Patented in 1801, the tourbillon remains a technical accomplishment that can only be achieved by a handful of exceptionally skilled watchmakers. Fewer than one thousand have been built in nearly two centuries.

One of Breguet's other major innovations was the "Souscription." Introduced during the economic depression following the Revolution, the "Souscription"

system was an exceptional idea, both in terms of technique and marketing. Moderately priced watches in small series were available for purchase under an installment system allowing the client to pay only one quarter of the total price at the time of order, and the balance during the execution of the timepiece. The process made the watches more affordable to an emerging "nouvelle bourgeoisie," while enabling the Maestro to finance his projects and devote himself to his inventions.

In a workshop journal entry, dated December 3, 1798, Breguet defined his philosophy of watchmaking excellence: "The balance spring must be in the same position, the size and number of turns must be the same, and the shape of the balance-spring stud and index must be identical, so that the eye is struck by a fundamental similarity. Likewise, the exterior: the size of the case, the dial, the signature — regardless of whether it is painted or engraved — must be similar and in the same position as the model. The hands, crystals, keys, each part must bear the maker's special characteristics. Once the eye becomes accustomed to this fundamental identity, the slightest defect and the best imitation are immediately recognizable. As a result, all of the products will be infinitely improved; the craftsmen will benefit from this experience and constantly improve their skills, drawing

FROM TOP TO BOTTOM

Presented during the 1996 Basle Fair, this new man's wristwatch in 18K yellow gold reveals a striking new face. On a silvered gold "guilloché" dial, the Roman numerals displaying the hours are positioned circumferentially instead of radially and the small seconds are indicated on a subdial at 6 o'clock. Animated by a hand-wound movement, the timepiece is water resistant up to 30 meters (100 feet).

The Breguet "Hora Mundi" features a self-winding movement with a centre second-hand and a date calendar at 6 o'clock. The base of the winding-crown allows selection of the desired time setting in one of the 24 time zones.

1
2
3

Technical refinement and classic design merge to perfection in these three tourbillon models in 18K yellow gold.

1.This hand-wound movement with a Breguet overcoil is entirely engraved by hand. The triple-arrow of the small second-hand is mounted on and driven by the tourbillon shaft. Making three 120° angles, the three arrows run clockwise along the 20 seconds semi-circle dial fitted on the upper part of the tourbillon carriage.

2.Entirely engraved by hand, this hand-wound movement with tourbillon features a power reserve indicator and an unusual 24-hour retrograde time display. The small second-hand is fitted on the tourbillon shaft, visible through an aperture at 6 o'clock. Note the extreme attention given to aesthetic details and the four different types of "guilloché" on the face.

3.The sophisticated architecture of a skeletonized hand-wound movement with tourbillon. The chapter ring and seconds semi-circle are in silvered gold hand-engraved on a rose-engine.

greater pleasure from their work… For any creation, one must constantly bear these fundamental maker's rules on construction in mind…"

As a result, his incredibly complex watches were presented with trademarks of simplistic elegance. His contemporaries, on the other hand, were producing highly ornamental cases, in various colors of gold, engraved or enameled with figures, or set with precious stones. Breguet cases were devoid of superfluous decoration, characterized by the simplicity of their lines and the detailed attention to finish. Understated dials remain a hallmark of a Breguet watch. Each production respects the founder's principles of workmanship and begins with a sheet of solid gold, engine-turned by hand, then silver-plated

in the same manner prescribed by Breguet two hundred years ago. Among Breguet's numerous contributions to watchmaking aesthetical standards is the "guilloché" pattern, also known as engine-turning or "barleycorn" motif, used on dials since the 1650s. Executed with a special lather called a rose-engine, the technique produces a matte, finely textured surface. The elegant pattern also had very practical qualities. It prevented reflections and glimmer on the dial, providing instead a muted, easy-to-read surface. Today only a few craftsmen still practice the art of fine manual engraving, known as "guillochage." Several methods of guillochage were used for Breguet dials as early as 1788, and each motif was named for its distinctive pattern.

Breguet left such an indelible imprint on watchmaking that many of his creations became part of the vocabulary of horologists' lingo. His famous blued steel, hollow-tipped "pomme" hands bear his name, as do the Breguet overcoil balance spring. Breguet also perfected Arabic numerals, still called "Breguet numerals," to make them more refined, elegant and easy to read.

Though Breguet lived and worked in Paris most of his life, he dealt extensively with craftsmen in the region of the Vallée de Joux, and depended on them for parts. Two centuries later, Breguet's design and technological innovations still live on in the company's new watch production center in l'Abbaye, a village in the same quiet Vallée de Joux , home to centuries of watchmaking history. The artisans at Montres Breguet, now owned by Investcorp, still strictly comply with the guidelines upon which Breguet founded the company. This policy encompasses Breguet's untiring perfectionism and mechanical astuteness. Signature designs are perpetuated, like the blue steel hands, the guilloché engraving and the fluted caseband. To identify each Breguet creation, a specifically assigned production number is marked on each watch. The number testifies to the time and work spent on its making, usually several years. It also allows the watch to be tracked throughout its existence, with a lifespan of a century or more.

1. The "Réserve de Marche" is another marvel in Breguet's unmistakable style: its automatic movement animates a power reserve indicator located at 11 o'clock, a date calendar with the phases and age of the moon.

2. Breguet's "Jubilé" Skeleton Watch designed for the 220th anniversary of the foundation of the House of Breguet in 1995. Limited to 75 examples, the "Jubilé" Skeleton has an automatic double barrel, self-winding, 25 jewel movement entirely skeletonized, hand engraved, numbered and signed by Breguet. Among the many sophisticated details of the model are its B-shaped rotor in 21K yellow gold, its linear anchor escapement, and its single metal balance wheel.

3. Breguet's 18K yellow gold perpetual "Equation du Temps" features a self-winding patented movement with power indicator and perpetual calendar showing the day, date, month and leap years. The calculation of the equation of time can be read between 1 and 2 o'clock.

1. The man's "Marine" in 18K yellow gold houses a self-winding movement driving a date calendar and a sweep second-hand. Its silvered gold dial "guilloché" on a rose-engine is a Breguet trademark. Water resistant up to 50 meters, the "Marine," characterized by its fluted caseband and protected crown, is attached to a sharkskin bracelet with a gold folding clasp.

2. "Marine" Chronograph in its intermediate size. In 18K yellow gold, its bezel, strap attachments and clasps are set with 105 diamonds weighing 1.13 carat. Animated by a self-winding movement with date calendar and small seconds displayed on the 6 o'clock subdial, this jeweled chronograph is a tribute to functional elegance with a mother-of-pearl dial, hand-engraved on a rose-engine.

3. The Lady's "Marine" in 18K yellow gold. This version is set with diamonds on the bezel and bracelet attachments. Eleven diamonds serve as hour markers while the aperture for the date replaces the 6 o'clock marker.

1

2

3

RIGHT

The Type XX Aéronavale with its striking polished steel case, matt-black dial, tritium-coated hands and graduated rotating bezel, features a chronograph with fly-back function and two counters for 30-minutes and 12-hours chronographic time. The Type XX was first developed in the early 1950s for French Navy flyers.

Because each watch takes a considerable amount of time to complete, a policy of limited production enables Breguet to offer a wide range of models in limited series. There are now three lines of Breguet watches: Classic, Marine, and Type XX Aéronavale. The elegant Classic watch can be ultra-thin, hand-wound or self-winding, with an wide array of complications such as the column-wheel chronograph, the jumping hour, the tourbillon or the perpetual equation of time, indicating the variance between real and mean solar time. All watches in this line reflect the extreme technical and aesthetic criteria defined by Breguet.

Among the most impressive models are a perpetual calendar with an openwork tourbillon movement engraved by hand, displaying the mechanism within a transparent case, and the unique "Equation of Time" with its perpetual calendar and power reserve indicator.

Breguet's "Marine" watches are modern-day heirs to the nautical timepieces supplied by Breguet to the French Royal Navy in 1815. Engraved with the inscription "Horloger de la Marine," the contemporary "Marine" watches are water-resistant, dependable and rugged, sturdily constructed with a reinforced case and a protected ogive-shaped winding crown with a signed Breguet ring.

The "Marine" jewelry watches for ladies are dazzling, harmoniously featuring diamonds and precious gemstones inserted in white or yellow gold cases and bracelets, with iridescent mother-of-pearl dials.

To calibrate its historical link between aeronautics and watchmaking, in 1995 the firm reissued Breguet's Type XX Aéronavale initially developed in the 1950s for the French Navy flyers. The new version retains all the essential features of its original, including a black dial, a graduated rotating bezel, and the famous *"retour en vol"* or fly-back function, which returns the chronograph-hand to zero and restarts it immediately at the single touch of a button.

Until he passed away in 1823, Breguet continued to explore new ways to master time. In his eulogy, Charles Dupin, a member of the French Royal Academy of Sciences, declared: "Not all who mourn your death are present here: the entire motherland will experience regret at your loss, because you contributed to the triumph of [your] Art."

To every watchmaker since, Breguet has been the man who not only measured, but challenged time by revolutionizing the science of horology and the art of watchmaking. Further enhanced by his successors at the company that bears his name, Breguet's achievements remain as relevant and ravishing as ever.

1

2

3

4

1. Breguet's lady's watch in 18K yellow gold. Its fluted case is fitted with a hand-wound movement, numbered and signed Breguet. Its attachments and bezel are set with 80 diamonds and 5 cabochon rubies on the crown and on each of the attachment sides. Its case is water resistant up to 30 meters.

2. Lady's "Marine" watch in 18K rose gold with automatic movement. Its bezel attachments and central links of the bracelet are set with 197 baguette-shape Top Wesselton diamonds, weighing 14.70 carats. Its face is paved with 183 brilliants and adorned with 11 indexes in sapphire. This watchmaking jewel is water resistant up to 30 meters.

3. Lady's "Marine" watch in 18K yellow gold with diamonds and cabochon sapphire crown. Its bezel, attachments and bracelet are entirely set with 212 diamonds and 74 trapeze and baguette-shaped diamonds weighing approximately 9.2 carats.

4. Lady's "Marine" watch in 18K yellow gold with self-winding movement, date calendar and sweep seconds. The bezel, attachments and bracelet are entirely set with 212 diamonds and 74 trapeze and baguette-shaped rubies.

The cultural heritage of the House of Cartier began in 1847 when Louis-François Cartier (1819-1904), after first serving as an apprentice, acquired the workshop of master jeweler Adolphe Picard. With Napoléon II's 1856 takeover of France, Paris regained its previous gaiety. Elegance and luxury swirled through the many fêtes and balls. The splendors of the Second Empire provided an ideal environment in which the new Cartier business could flourish. Louis-François became a friend of the internationally-known couturier, Charles Worth, and this encounter would be the beginning of a long-

Jacques and Pierre, started branches in London and New York. Louis' genius for design innovation made him a leader of the Art Déco period of the 1920's. In this fertile period of creation, he designed distinctive watches and clocks garnished with clever features and technical accomplishments, such as the brilliant "mystery clocks" now found in the world's greatest museums. Cartier attained patents for many of these features. Louis also collaborated with master horologist Maurice Coüet, to develop luxury timepieces like the six famous Cartier "Portico" clocks. During this creatively prolific

Cartier

lasting friendship. The families were eventually united by marriages: first between Louis Cartier and Andrée Worth in 1898, and later between Louis' sister Suzanne Cartier and Jacques Worth. This alliance and prestigious patronage added to the growth of Cartier's fame. In 1867, Louis-François Cartier exhibited his jewelry at the Paris World Fair, winning wide acclaim. The success was immediate, and by 1888, Cartier began to make his first timepieces. In 1899, Louis-François' grandson, Louis Cartier, took over Cartier Paris on Rue de La Paix at the age of twenty-three. Meanwhile his two brothers,

time, Louis' friend Alberto Santos-Dumont, the stylish Brazilian aviator bemoaned the inconvenience of fumbling for his pocket watch while trying to pilot his craft. In response, Louis designed and dedicated the first Cartier wristwatch to Santos-Dumont in 1904. Since then, the "Santos" has remained one of Cartier's most successful designs. Six years later, Louis cleverly added to his model the "déployant" buckle, a folding clasp which snapped the watch to the wrist. In the 1920's Cartier's reputation took Louis across the frontiers of Europe.

ABOVE LEFT

The "Belle Epoque" bracelet watch by Cartier in 1910. Made in platinum, the square-shaped watch displays a rose diamond case and rose diamond winding crown. Its bracelet is made of 4 rows of pearls with a buckle inserted with diamonds.

ABOVE RIGHT

The "Panthère" bracelet watch in gold presented by Cartier in 1926 features the "Panthère" style watch with 18K yellow gold bracelet and deployant buckle on a white dial with the famous Cartier black roman numerals.

RIGHT

The diamond "Baignoire" watch by Cartier circa 1920. The platinum baignoire case is surrounded by diamonds and onyx with rose diamond winding crown, silvered dial, and pearl bracelet.

PREVIOUS PAGE

The Tank Française square-shaped 18K yellow gold watch on an leather strap, introduced in 1996. Available in three sizes, in a variety of movements ranging from quartz to the automatic mechanical to split-second chronograph movement with perpetual calendar and automatic time zone changing capability.

He catered to the needs of Russia's nobility, organizing several trips and exhibitions in St. Petersburg.

Louis surrounded himself with gifted designers, such as Charles Jacqueau, and opened the House of Cartier to many influences from Persian, Egyptian and Oriental styles. Louis brought new accents and harmony to his creations, combining traditional designs with exotic inspirations, all displaying the Cartier style. The popularity of Cartier wristwatches was boosted in 1906 with the introduction of Cartier jeweled wristwatches, which supported the growing success of the "Santos" watch.

In 1917, Louis Cartier created what many believe is the single most important and influential watch design of the 20th century, the legendary Cartier "Tank" watch, designed as a tribute to the Allied tank commanders who helped defend France in World War I. This slim watch, with its elegantly curved profile, continues to be a worldwide status symbol to this day.

In 1926, Jeanne Toussaint came to the House of Cartier. For the next fifty years, she served as collaborator, muse and creator. She managed the S Department, created in 1923 for the design of luxury accessories. The new S Department was set up to extend the Cartier collection to a wider public. It became a forerunner of today's "Les Must de Cartier."

In 1933, the Pasha of Marrakesh commissioned Cartier to create a watch that he might wear while swimming in his garden pools. Inspired by the challenge, Cartier designed one of the earliest water-resistant watches, a new frontier in horology. The first "Pasha" watch with its famous water-resistant round case was made of solid gold. The elegant model would become the perfect watch for collectors who seek a rare and precious timepiece.

In 1962, after the deaths of all the Cartier brothers, the firm was broken into three pieces and sold by the estate to different owners in Paris, in London, and in New York. Ten years would pass before three visionaries, Robert Hocq, Alain-Dominique Perrin, and Joseph Kanoui, would bring the three branches back together once again.

With the establishing of "Les Must de Cartier" in 1973, Alain-Dominique Perrin has created a network of Cartier stores and boutiques in over 120 countries. The company's watch designers continue to draw on the rich design archives left behind by Louis Cartier, and from that vast resource has come such current Cartier watch models as the "Panther," the "Baignoire," the "Pasha," the "Tonneau," and the "Diabolo."

The company's latest achievement is the "Tank Française." Based on the famous design of the Tank created in 1917,

TOP LEFT

The "Tonneau" watch by Cartier circa 1912. The large model with the famous 18K yellow gold barrel-shaped case and silvered guilloché dial.

TOP RIGHT

The "Tank" watch by Cartier circa 1920 in 18K yellow gold with 2 lines of black enamel on the case.

CENTER

The "Tank" watch with Taxi dial by Cartier in 1928. The impressive jumping-hour is made of 18K yellow gold with its winding stem on the lower edge.

BOTTOM LEFT

The "Baignoire" watch with leaf motif bracelet. Made of white gold with round diamonds and 16 cultured pearls, it features a mother-of-pearl dial. The total diamond weight is 7.29 cts.

RIGHT

The "Cloche" watch by Cartier circa 1920 features a 18K yellow gold bell-shaped case with a white dial and a cabochon sapphire crown.

ABOVE LEFT

The Cartier jeweled watch collection pictured clockwise:

- *The diamond "Tank Obux" with a red strap features 157 pavé diamonds on its bezel and case. Available on a strap or 18K gold bracelet.*
- *The diamond "Diabolo" is spectacularly adorned with a total of 1,636 pavé diamonds on the dial, bezel, case and bracelet.*
- *The diamond "Tank Americaine" comes in several sizes for ladies and gentlemen, ranging from the smaller 99 pavé diamonds to the larger 103 pavé diamonds version.*
- *The diamond "Panther" watch with its Art Déco bracelet presents a strong contrast of geometric shapes realized by 144 pavé diamonds and gold links. Another 45 pavé diamonds embrace the opalescent dial.*

ABOVE RIGHT

The "Tank Americaine" watch is available in a complete range for men and women, in both quartz and mechanical movements and water-resistant to 100 feet.

RIGHT

The "Tank Cintrée" circa 1924 in platinum with sapphire winding crown.

the "Tank Française" is a model of horology and design mastery, displaying elegance and diversity.

Available in three sizes, the square-shaped model offers a variety of movements from quartz to automatic with features ranging from split-second chronograph with perpetual calendar to automatic time zone changing capability.

In 1991, under the direction of Mr. Perrin, Cartier assumed a leadership role among Swiss watchmakers when it organized a major new watch fair at which only timepieces at the luxury level could be presented. The fair, called the Salon International de la Haute Horlogerie (SIHH), is now held each spring in Geneva and introduces Cartier's newest jewelry watches and limited-edition jeweled clocks to buyers and connoisseurs from around the world.

Many of the great horological masterpieces Cartier has created over the years have been prominently featured by museums all over the world. Major retrospectives called *The Art of Cartier* have been presented at the Petit Palais in Paris, The Hermitage in St. Petersburg, The Metropolitan Museum of Art in New York, The Los Angeles County Museum of Art, among others.

Marvels of technology and design, these Pasha are genuine watchmaking masterpieces.

On the right, the Pasha with Phases of the Moon features a spectacular guilloché dial in rosace pattern inserted in an 18K yellow gold base.

On the left, the Pasha Perpetual Calendar includes additional functions with the phases of the moon and leap years. The guilloché dial shows a wave pattern. All Pasha models features the most recognizable cabochon crown in sapphire. These two models have transparent skeleton back with visible oscillating mass in 18K yellow gold.

Recent years have seen the publication of a number of major books celebrating the achievements of the House, among them *Cartier: Jewelers Extraordinaire* (Abrams, 1984), *Le Temps de Cartier* (Wrist Int'l, 1989), *Made by Cartier* (Mondadori, 1992), and *Platinum by Cartier* (Abrams, 1996.) While each book highlights a different aspect of the Cartier heritage, collectively these works give eloquent testimony to the richness and historical importance of Cartier's creativity and prestige.

Year after year, the House of Cartier continues to create new timepieces of great distinction with a regularity that seems deceptively effortless.

ABOVE

The "Gouvernail" watch in 1948. An 18K yellow gold helm-shaped case with white dial and Breguet hands.

RIGHT

The "Tortue" chronograph watch circa 1928. An 18K yellow gold model with silvered dial and a traditional winding crown.

Keeping time with tradition for more than 135 years, Chopard's history quietly started in the small Swiss village of Sonvilier, on the road from St. Imier to La Chaux-de-Fonds. In this region known for its bleak winters, biting winds and watchmaking "comptoirs," twenty-four year old Louis-Ulysse Chopard became an independent watchmaker in 1860. Producing the finest in pocket watches, Chopard's pieces, all bearing his initials "L.U.C.," quickly gained recognition for their extreme reliability and precision. To counter the uncertainties of the Industrial Revolution, in 1912 Louis-Ulysse Chopard boldly decided to

Louis-Ulysse's grandson, Paul-André, decided that the company's efforts should be concentrated on the creation of luxury timepieces. Having no descendant willing to carry on the enterprise his grandfather had founded, Chopard needed a solvent and solid successor, or the company was doomed... Owner of the respected Pforzheim-based company Eszeha watches, German watchmaker Karl Scheufele was looking to work independently from Swiss watch movement producers. Interested in the company, he came to Paul-André Chopard. Both men soon realized that their interests coincided, and in 1963 the

explore new markets and traveled East through Poland and Hungary and finally "conquered" the Court of Russia. The trip gave his order book a major boost, and in the 1920s he packed his tools to relocate in a small house in Geneva. Known for his high quality watches, the precision of his timepieces was so impressive that he also became a major supplier to the *Chemins de Fer Helvétiques* – Switzerland's Railroads – a company well known for its punctuality. Unfortunately, quality timepieces and ancillary business propositions were not enough to secure the future of the Chopard legacy. By the early 1960s,

Scheufele family acquired Chopard, vowing to maintain the firm's commitment to quality. It was a daring purchase, as the sixties and seventies threatened Swiss watchmaking with competition from the Far East, mainly Japan. However, against all odds, Karl Scheufele, with the help of his wife Karin and their watchmakers managed to revive the company with the support of Paul-André Chopard, who smoothed the transition and continued making hand-fashioned pocket chronometers before passing away five years later. Under the new management, changes were rapidly made to allow for future growth.

1. The Chopard family with, from right
to left, Louis-Ulysse Chopard, his
son Paul, and his grandsons Jean
and Paul-André.

2. Chopard's "Mille Miglia" line
of sports watches came into
existence with Karl-Friedrich
Scheufele's personal contribution to
the resurrection of the "Mille Miglia"
race. The line features sports timers,
chronographs, exclusive wristwatches
and a line of accessories specially
created for the race. Displayed below
are three ladies' jewelry watch
versions. Their bezels are inserted
with diamonds, sapphires, rubies and
emeralds.

PREVIOUS PAGE

Sophistication and sparkle of precious
stones of Chopard's latest collection.

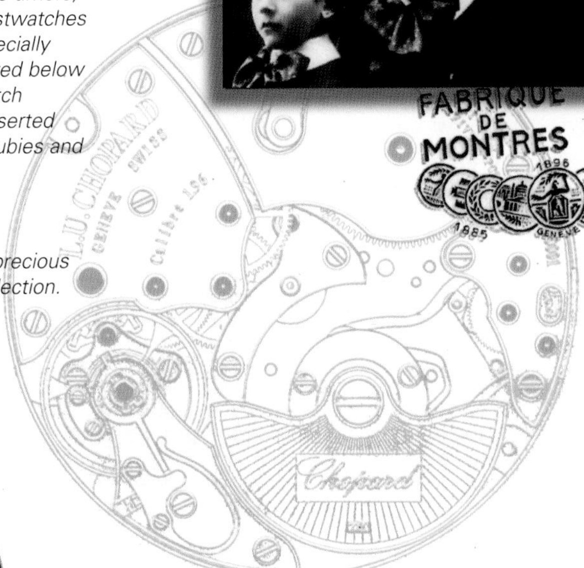

In 1972 the company relocated to an ultra-modern facility in Meyrin, a suburb of Geneva. Today, Chopard is one of the most modern watch manufacturers with an impressive production capacity. Its own Watchmaking Training Center, founded in 1991, emphasizes the high claims made by Chopard in "Haute Horlogerie." There, specialists in the repair and maintenance of Chopard timepieces from around the world are invited to complete a series of training courses.

The building also houses a 400 square meters watch museum. The museum is a testimony to the House of Chopard's history, featuring selections from each of the company's major lines and early examples of watchmaking tools and workbenches. The Museum showcases the complete collection of pocket watches and wrist-watches of two makes, Eszeha from Profzheim and Chopard from Sonvilier and Geneva. A showcase dedicated to counterfeit Chopard watches demonstrates the distinction between fake and authentic creations, emphasizing the exceptional skills required to make a genuine Chopard watch. These high standards are assured today by the entire Scheufele family: Karl Scheufele, his wife Karin, and their two children Karl-Friedrich and Caroline. Chopard is one of few watch companies of international importance which is still run as a traditional family business.

Chopard's success story is unique in many ways. From its two production sites in Geneva and Pforzheim, and its new movement manufacture in Fleurier, Chopard distributes its lines to its five subsidiaries in France, Italy, Austria, Spain and the United States. Exclusive boutiques have been established in Geneva, Athens, Baden-Baden, London, Paris, Vienna, New York, Dubai, Hong Kong, Jakarta, Kuala Lumpur, Osaka, Singapore, Taipei and Tokyo. A latest addition will be the opening of a Chopard Boutique in Moscow in January 1997. Karl Scheufele attributes the company's global expansion to the efforts Chopard has made to cater to people of many different tastes with a line of more than 450 models in various styles and materials, and to a "personal approach and service to the client." The company's eight in-house designers create 150 new models every year. Chopard produces today an astonishing 30,000 watches – and 15,000 pieces of jewelry – compared with only a few hundred just 25 years ago.

To achieve this success, Chopard links the past, present and future, utilizing technological advances such as Computer Assisted Design (CAD) while maintaining strict attention to detail, precision, and quality craftsmanship. Thus, a Chopard watch is guaranteed to be an exclusive, original, in-house product.

1. A declaration of understated elegance, this 18K yellow gold case, water-resistant to 30 meters, holds an automatic double-going spring barrel movement with a power reserve of 100 hours. On a white face marked with black roman numerals, the small seconds and the date can be read on the subdial at 6 o'clock.

2. Inside this polished 18K rose gold case, water-resistant up to 30 meters, is a mechanical movement driving hour and minute hands on a silvered dial with gold hour-markers, and small seconds on the subdial at 6. The movement can be admired through a sapphire crystal caseback.

3. The Automatic Perpetual Calendar in 18K yellow gold indicates the phases of the moon at 6, and the date on an offset half-circle at 12. The days of the week are on a subdial at 9, around the 24-hour counter. The months are on the subdial at 3, surrounding the leap-year cycle where the bissextile year is marked by a red "4". Hour and minute hands are luminous, indicating the time on white gold markers. This timepiece comes in gold or platinum.

4. Produced in limited series, the "Mille Miglia Chrono-stop" is carved out of stainless steel or solid 18K gold, and fully complies with the ambition to create highly accurate timepieces of lasting value.

5. In its present form, the "Mille Miglia," as a race between classic vintage automobiles, has taken place every year since 1977 in northern and central Italy. In 1988, Karl-Friedrich Scheufele, under the Chopard name, decided to become the main sponsor of the resurrected and now extremely popular event. To support him, his father Karl and sister Caroline.

Chopard's jewelry timepieces are inspired by the jewels that are to be showcased in the piece itself. Precious stones were also the inspiration for Chopard's most popular ladies' line, the "Happy Diamonds" collection, which celebrates its 20th anniversary this year. The prototype for this line, which now includes watches, jewelry, decorative pieces and perfumes, earned Chopard the "Golden Rose of Baden-Baden" award in 1976. The idea came to designer Ronald Kurowski as he was hiking through the German Black Forest. Coming across a waterfall, he was entranced by the movement of water droplets gracefully plunging onto the rocks below.

Back at his drawing board, this feat of nature led him to experiment with small, unmounted brilliants. "Brilliants first reveal their beauty and their fire when they move," Kurowski says. To emulate the free-falling dew drops, he created a setting that would give diamonds freedom of movement within a sapphire-glass case. "Diamonds would look happy," he explains, "if they were left to dance, to move around within the circle of a watch, sparkling and reflecting the light like drops of water." Chopard produced several variations of the original "Happy Diamonds" model, such as the new "Happy Sport" collection. Seven free-spinning diamonds tumble across the face of a sporty watch. A limited-edition model of the "Happy Sport" has been created in celebration of the line's twentieth anniversary. "Happy Diamonds" have been extremely popular among patrons of Chopard. Because of the overwhelming success of the "Happy Diamonds" line, Chopard is now primarily known for its specialty women's watches. Its "Alta Moda" and "La Vie en Rose" are described as lines created from "pure gems for women who love beautiful jewels." "La Vie en Rose," introduced in 1994, is a line dedicated to the romance of Paris, as immortalized by the voice of French chanteuse Edith Piaf. Called "a hymn to passion," the watches are adorned with fancy pink Australian diamonds, and fastened with pink or red crocodile leather straps. "The combination," says the company, "lends tenderness and feminity to the passing of time." Chopard's latest collection is a whole jewelry line including watches, bracelets, earrings, necklaces and rings. The 18K gold of the watches can be set with square-cut diamonds, rubies, emeralds or sapphires on the inner links of the bracelet, while the outer links are studded with pink or white diamonds. The design rises from the 1950s, with a rectangular face set with diamonds as well. The Collection recollects a time of youth and stylish innocence.

ABOVE

Three magnificent pieces from the "Happy Sport" Collection: in white or yellow gold, with seven mobile white diamonds sparkling on the face, and ruby, sapphire or emerald cabochons on the winding crown and bracelet attachments.

RIGHT

The "Happy Diamonds 20th Anniversary" limited edition. Only 1996 pieces will be produced. To commemorate the anniversary, the 12 o'clock index says "XX."

1. The "Tonneau Small Seconds" in an 18K yellow gold variant, is powered by a mechanical movement.
The 18K gold "Tonneau Réserve de Marche." Its case, water resistant to 30 meters, houses an automatic movement with a power reserve of 45 hours indicated at 3. Its elegant face displays a silvered "guilloché" dial, with applied gold roman numerals.

2. One of the models originating from the "Mille Miglia" collection, this 18K gold chronograph is accurate to one fifth of a second, and is coupled to a tachymetric scale. Recording elapsed time on its 30-minute and 12-hour counters, its automatic movement also activates a date indicator located at 3 o'clock and the small seconds on the counter at 12. Next to it, the Automatic with date and small seconds.

To the right, the Automatic Perpetual Calendar in 18K yellow gold with its two double-function subdials: at 3, the months and leap-year cycle with the bissextile year marked with a red "4," and at 9, the 24-hour counter and the days of the week. The offset semi-circle at 12 indicates the date while the phases of the moon can be read at 6.

Chopard's designs are also meant for the sports enthusiast. Introduced in 1980, the "St. Moritz" line was called "the pioneer" for breaking with tradition. Recently, the company introduced the St. Moritz II. Water resistant to 100 meters, the model now comes with an automatic LeCoultre movement. While the rim has a classic round form, its characteristic eight screws give the watch an elegant, high-class yet robust look. The name suits the watch because it brings to mind "Switzerland, sports and the upper class." The feminine "Gstaad" line, introduced six years later, was designed by Caroline Scheufele herself. Each watch distinctively captures the essence of fashionable sports, long associated with the famous Gstaad resort.

In 1988, the "Mille Miglia" collection was created as an homage to the thrilling recreation of road racing, a passion shared by Karl Scheufele and his son. The two found inspiration when taking an exhilarating drive in Italy's "Mille Miglia" vintage car race. "We could clearly identify with these rare collector's items, symbols of superior engineering, workmanship and aesthetics," said Karl-Friedrich Scheufele. "This led us to create a series of classic timepieces that reflect our dedication to excellence, innovative design and technical perfection." This dedication is the idea behind the "Mille Miglia" line, which features precision chronographs and sports timers in solid gold and stainless steel.

On a more traditional side, Chopard offers an impressive collection of classic and complicated timepieces as well: with its understated elegance, the "Chopard Tonneau" line, with its stylish patterns of *guilloché* on the face, exemplifies the perfect balance between style and technical prowess. Reviving the popular *tonneau* shape of the 1920s, the line offers a hand-wound model with small seconds, an automatic Perpetual Calendar and an automatic with *Réserve de Marche* indicator. Both models are available in 18K yellow, white and pink gold, or 950 platinum. Other classics include the round automatic ultra-thin "Musée," available with a date calendar, or the rectangular hand-wound "Dual Time." These models are the latest in a family tree going back to the 1930s. Their modern improvements include automatic movements, scratch resistant sapphire glass and water resistant cases. Skeleton movements show their intricate beauty through gold or platinum cases. Established in 1996, the "Chopard Manufacture S.A." in Fleurier produces brand name movements, such as the automatic movement L.U.C. 1/96. From 1996 onwards, 2,000 "Haut de Gamme" movements are to be made annually.

Chopard's future is secure in the hands of the Scheufele family. Caroline is expanding the company's lines with creative new pieces. Karl-Friedrich plans to oversee the rise of even more mechanical innovations, exclaiming, "There is still a lot to be done."

The "Imperiale" Chronograph Collection.

1. Matching the red crocodile strap, the 18K yellow gold is enhanced with red ruby cabochons on the crown, the octagonal push buttons of the chronograph, and the strap attachments. The aperture of the date indicator is located at 4:30.

2. The bezel, bracelet and dial of this chronograph are set with 444 diamonds weighing 10.20 carats, while the push buttons, crown and bracelet attachments are fitted with seven sapphire cabochons.

3. Chopard pieces are designed around precious stones. The colors for the dials, cases and bracelets are carefully chosen to match these mineral marvels, such as these emeralds or sapphires.

4. The bezel is set with 20 diamonds of equal size. These precious stones look even more startling on the golden bed of the case. The hour markers are also set with little brilliants. The blue on the three subdials matches the sapphires on the crown, push buttons and strap holders.

In 1887, Georges-Emile Eberhard founded his "Manufacture Suisse d'Horlogerie", and from that day on set out to make history. Not only did he keep up with his time, a minimum for a professional in his field, but he was often ahead of it, earning his reputation as watchmaker extraordinaire in the utterly exclusive club of world famous Swiss watch master craftsmen. From his headquarters in La Chaux-de-Fonds, in the Canton of Neuchâtel – one of Switzerland's centers of watchmaking – his business grew steadily. His circle of buyers, from crowned heads to the glitterati and military

masterpieces like the "Chronomaster," stamped with the Italian Air Force's "Frecce Tricolori" emblem; the "Maréoscope" with its dual tide indicator; the famous "Tazio Nuvolari" chronograph dedicated to the "Flying Mantovanian;" the "Scafomaster" that will gladly go down an incredible 1500 feet below the shimmering surface of the ocean, all testify to Eberhard & Co.'s omnipresence. From the Abyss all the way up to the Heavens, Eberhard has a watch for all adventures. The success of Eberhard & Co. is based on several directing lines: an elaborate list of requirements met through exhaustive

Eberhard

forces, widened to include all of Europe, the Middle East, and finally the Americas and Asia. Eberhard's enterprise was prolific, not only because of its growing clientele, but most of all for what fascinated them, his technical "Tours de Force." No time was lost: 1919 was the year of his wristwatch chronograph, one of the most sophisticated of its time. 1930 was the year of his first automatic watch, followed in 1935 by the Dual push-button chronograph and in 1939 the "Rattrapante" chronograph. Still in the thirties, the Eberhard chronographs were worn on the wrists of the Italian Royal Navy officers. Today,

research, inventiveness in development, extra attention to the most minute detail, and stringent testing. Eberhard's passion for detail is felt not only in the technical achievements, but also in the aesthetics of its timepieces. The use and work of precious metals enhance the delicately shaped parts of each model, like the finely pearlized gold on the case and bezel of the Quadrangolo, or the tiny beads of gold set in the shiny steel winding crown of the Chronomaster models. With its famed Tazio Nuvolari, steel itself, pearlized on the bezel and caseback, and polished to a shine on the chronograph push-buttons, becomes precious metal.

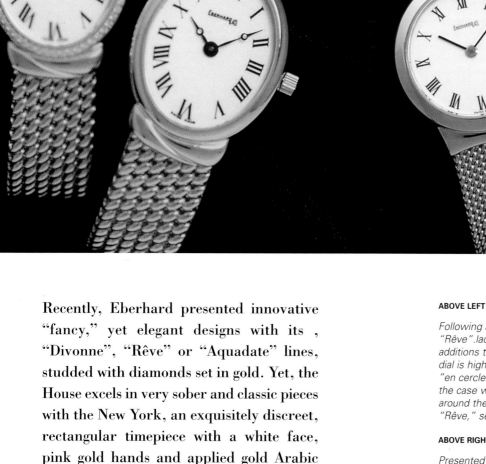

Recently, Eberhard presented innovative "fancy," yet elegant designs with its , "Divonne", "Rêve" or "Aquadate" lines, studded with diamonds set in gold. Yet, the House excels in very sober and classic pieces with the New York, an exquisitely discreet, rectangular timepiece with a white face, pink gold hands and applied gold Arabic numerals in a pink gold case. The supreme elegance of this watch resides in its refined simplicity, and its smooth, sensual, rounded edges.

Ever since the House was founded more than a hundred years ago, its quest for technical excellence, refined quality and composed elegance never wavered. "Méchanisme & Tradition" is what you will find, under the name "Eberhard & Co."

ABOVE LEFT

Following a tradition of understated elegance, the "Rêve".ladies' watches are some of Eberhard & Co's latest additions to its "Bracelets Or" Collection. Its pure white dial is highlighted by black Roman numerals and hands "en cercle." The tiny gold links of the bracelet attached to the case with "wrapped" gold, form a delicate chain around the wrist. Even more striking is the bejeweled "Rêve," set with diamonds on the bezel.

ABOVE RIGHT

Presented at the 1996 Basle Fair, the "Divonne" is another superlative in daintiness. Made of polished 18K yellow gold, it can also be set with diamonds on the bezel.

UPPER RIGHT

The classical and sophisticated lines of the "Hyperbole." This tonneau-shaped stainless steel case in two parts, water-resistant, holds a self-winding movement. This rugged soul inside a refined body is at home anywhere, from golf courses to black tie occasions. The elongated black Roman numerals and black straight hands on a white face make it an extremely refined timepiece.

Amidst the turbulent era of the late 18th century, Jean-Marc Vacheron steadily developed and improved his craft as a master watchmaker, but not without his own personal troubles. Little is documented from the first fifty years of the Vacheron Constantin history. However, Genevan archives reveal that, in 1755, Jean-Marc Vacheron, together with an apprentice, established a new workshop in the quarter of Saint-Gervais, and was forced to borrow "1,000 pounds of silver" to finance the first steps of the new venture. An avid reader of pamphlets and political treatises, Jean-Marc Vacheron followed

Overcoming the agonies of the Revolution, the collapse of trade routes, riots and hunger, the three Vacheron master-watchmakers, Jean-Marc and his sons, Louis André and Abraham, managed to survive and expand. Indeed, the Manufactory benefitted from Napoleon's blockade, which excluded the English watch industry from international trade, thus giving Geneva free reign in continental Europe. The old continent was in ruins when, in 1810, Jacques-Barthelemy Vacheron took over the reins of the family business. Success remained unstable in the opening years of the new century,

Vacheron Constantin

the social and political developments of this tumultuous century, while diligently pursuing his profession as "Cabinotier," combining his fascination for world affairs with the creation of horological masterpieces. At the time, Vacheron was one of the eight hundred Genevan "Cabinotiers" who were earning a living for their horological mastery: "It was more than a speciality, it was a fever, an obsession for measuring time." In this environment, Vacheron's limited production, remarkable for its quality and elegance, quickly attracted the attention of the French and Italian aristocracies.

but by 1813, Vacheron started working with the renowned watchmaker Breguet, taking Paris by storm with creations and technical marvels. Vacheron was soon commissioned to create pieces for the King of Rome - Napoleon's son. In 1819, rural disaster once again afflicted the industry in Geneva, and a two-year economic depression ensued. However, on April 1, 1819, Jacques-Barthelemy Vacheron took a decisive step which was to change the face of destiny. In forming a partnership with François Constantin, he established the name which has symbolized the company ever since.

JEAN-MARC VACHERON
1731 * 1805

FRANÇOIS CONSTANTIN
1788 - 1854

ILLUSTRATIONS ABOVE

Manuscript of technical instructions for the manufacture of a Vacheron Constantin watch in 1870.

The famous watchmaker's workshop. The image which perpetuates Vacheron Constantin's dedication to traditional watchmaking. A painting by Christophe François de Ziegler.

The Girod-Vacheron workshops in 1812 at the Tour de l'Isle in Geneva.

PREVIOUS PAGE

The splendid women's gem set "Fiorenza" watch from Vacheron Constantin's "Les Absolues" line. The tonneau-shaped case and "crescent moon" style bracelet in 18K yellow gold are set with 442 diamonds totaling 5.04 carats. The dial is paved with 106 diamonds weighing .39 carats.

The partnership gave the company a great boost. It enabled Vacheron to concentrate on his watchmaking talents in Geneva, while Constantin was traveling the roads of Europe on horseback with his saddlebag full of horological treasures. Constantin was renowned for his ebullient personality. Anecdotes record that he was often drawn into duels to defend the honor of his company, and climbed Italian mountain passes armed with swords and pistols. Constantin vowed that he was ready to defend himself against ruffians whose numbers grew in proportion to the political insecurity of the country. He was responsible for establishing Vacheron Constantin's network of contacts and clients in international markets. This trade caused constant struggles with custom officials and excisemen until the doctrine of free-trade finally began to be accepted. However, even prior to the official establishment of free trade in the 1840s, Vacheron Constantin already distributed watches in countries as far away as Rio de Janeiro, Stockholm, Malta, Liverpool, the United States, the Far East and Russia.

The company was infinitely strengthened by Constantin, whose personality and superb public relations allowed him to charm his way into the best salons of Europe. As a result, Vacheron was commissioned to create the most exquisite horological creations for dukes, counts, princes and ambassadors in all the palaces of Europe. In the early 19th century, Europe found herself in the throes of post-revolutionary decadence. The pursuit of luxury and leisure among the aristocracy suddenly became incredibly fashionable. Vacheron Constantin became the ultimate company to supply the ultimate accessory, the watch.

As the business expanded, Vacheron's heirs brought in a number of partners, whose talents proved invaluable to the success of the company. In 1839, Vacheron Constantin hired Georges-Auguste Leschot, a man who made an invaluable contribution to the company's reputation and capabilities. Leschot was a mechanical genius, who was to be remembered in the history of watchmaking and industrial development for his invention of practical equipment capable of producing watch parts. When he joined in 1839, Leschot accepted the challenge Vacheron and Constantin set him: to mechanically manufacture the components of their watches.

JUMPING HOUR IN PLATINUM

This replica of a design from the 1930's features a transparent sapphire back through which its self-winding mechanical movement can be seen. Under the silvered, engine-turned dial, hour figures are inscribed on a disc and "jumps every hour on the hour" by one twelfth of a complete rotation and are displayed in an aperture at 12 o'clock. A raised triangle, hand-tipped with onyx, sweeps around the dial to show the minutes on the rim of the dial.

SKELETON TOURBILLON IN ROSE GOLD

This skeleton tourbillon features a movement with twin series-coupled barrels. Its regulating unit, escapement and balance wheel are mounted in a tourbillon carriage which rotates on itself over one minute. Skeletonizing the movement required removing over 71% of the original metal before housing it in the 18K rose gold case. The sapphire dial is inscribed with Roman numerals and features a power-reserve indicator at 12. Vacheron Constantin's skeleton tourbillon is part of a limited series of only 300 to be produced.

PLATINUM TOURBILLON

The men's platinum Tourbillon features a movement with twin series-coupled barrels, with its regulating unit, escapement and balance wheel mounted in a tourbillon carriage. The silvered "guilloché" dial displays three roman numerals and six applied gold markers with a power reserve indicator at 12. Vacheron Constantin's Tourbillon Collection is limited to 300 tourbillon editions, including the skeleton tourbillon and the tourbillon in yellow gold.

In less than two years this exceptional man had built a range of machines capable of turning out any watch part in any size and perfectly adapted to the existing calibers. This realization revolutionized the small world of the "cabinotiers." Throughout the 19th century, Vacheron Constantin continued to develop its horological expertise, producing increasingly sophisticated designs and complicated timepieces. The company concentrated on establishing the strong principles of product quality which they still maintain today. Remaining of François Constantin's motto of the 19th century: "Do better if possible - and it is always possible," the company outgrew their old premises at Tour de l'Ile and decided to move to the opposite building on Quai des Moulins. Shortly afterwards, in 1880, Vacheron Constantin decided to adopt the Maltese Cross as its symbol, and to change the company name to "Vacheron & Constantin." The choice of the Maltese Cross was very significant. In the watchmaking industry, the Cross represented a small toothed wheel which adjusted the tension of the spring in old precision watches. For over 100 years the creations of Vacheron Constantin have borne this symbol which demonstrates their attachment to the Cabinotiers' values, their instruments and their ideas.

THE MERCATOR IN PLATINUM

Inspired by the founder of modern cartography, Gerardus Mercator, this limited edition features a choice of hand-chased dials with a map of the Americas or Europe, Asia and Africa. The hour and minute hands are fitted on an off centered axis and move over two graduated sectors in a "retrograde" time-display system. A complicated mechanism enabling the hands to be actuated on separate scales – 12 hours on the left and 60 minutes on the right. Water resistant to 30m and available 18K yellow gold and platinum, the Mercator features an automatic movement with power reserve.

Clockwise from top right

MINUTE REPEATER IN PLATINUM

This classic minute repeater replicates one of Vacheron Constantin's design from the late 1930's. It contains an amazingly thin hand-wound mechanical movement measuring 3.30 mm. With a 48-hour power reserve, it strikes the hours, quarters, and minutes at the press of a finger. Available with an 18K yellow gold or platinum case with a silvered dial bearing four roman numerals, hour markers and studs, and complemented by an engraved 18K gold case back and a sapphire crystal. Each of the 200 limited editions have a certificate of authenticity.

THE "52 WEEKER" IN YELLOW GOLD

Water resistant to 30 meters, the men's 18K yellow gold self-winding wristwatch displays a simple calendar: the day, date, week and phases of the moon. While the hour and minute hands provide the precise time, the week is shown by a crescent-tipped pointer sweeping around the dial. The day and date are provided by a pair of subdials and a rotating disc shows the phases of the moon.

PERPETUAL CALENDAR CHRONOGRAPH

In 18K pink gold, the timepiece features a self-winding mechanical movement including a 12-hour and 30-minute totalizer. The model also displays an auxiliary plate for the perpetual calendar that shows the day, date and month, automatically adjusting for months with 28, 29, 30 or 31 days. A moon phase indicator doubles as a subdial for the seconds. The chronograph timing operations and all adjustments can be effected by two push pieces and four correctors on the rim of the case. Water resistant, this version is presented with a white dial with gold hour markers and studs.

Today, the Maltese Cross still testify that each piece manufactured by Vacheron Constantin, is created "in respect of fine horology and the ethics that the enterprise has been defending since 1755."

Vacheron Constantin has one of the industry's most extensive and impressive line of "complicated" timepieces. "Les Complications" range from the understated, stylish wristwatch to the fabulous Grande Complication. Vacheron Constantin's "Les Complications" collection offers timepieces which are mechanically, and visually stunning: tourbillons, minute repeaters, jumping hours, perpetual calendars, chronographs and some unique creations such as the "Mercator." This model features a specially designed self-winding movement which comprises a complicated mechanism enabling the hands to be actuated on separate scales – 12 hours on the left and 60 minutes on the right.

As part of "Les Complications" line, a collection of pocket watches includes the classically stylish and technical "chef d'oeuvre," the "Grande Complication." With handwound, 20-line movement, the watch was entirely restored by Vacheron Constantin's watchmakers.

From left to right, top to bottom

"LES HISTORIQUES" MEN'S 18K YELLOW GOLD

This classic timepiece features a self-winding mechanical movement inserted in a round, angled case with horn-shaped lugs and a silvered "guilloché" dial with four Arabic numerals and eight gold markers.

"LES HISTORIQUES" CALENDAR WATCH

This 18K yellow gold automatic watch features a silvered, engine-turned dial with three gold Arabic and triangular markers. A double window under the 12 o'clock, displays the days of the week and the month, while the days of the month are featured around the dial and indicated by a crescent-tipped pointer. The moon phase indicator is located at 6 o'clock.

"LES HISTORIQUES" WOMEN

The 18K yellow gold cushion shaped watch circa 1950's presents a hand-wound mechanical movement encased in a square step down case with basket weave bracelet and a curved sapphire crystal. The elegant face displays a silvered dial with engine turned design center and raised square and triangular markers.

"LES HISTORIQUES" CHRONOGRAPH

This men's 18K yellow gold classic chronograph features a subdial for the seconds at 9 o'clock and a 30-minute totalizer at 3 o'clock. Its hand-wound mechanical movement can be observed through the clear sapphire back. The dial is silvered with a tachymetric scale bearing both Arabic numerals and hour markers.

It features a chronograph mechanism, a perpetual calendar fitted on an additional movement plate along with a minute repeater, 12-hour and 30-minute totalizer. It also possesses a highly-advanced calendar which shows the day of the week, the month, date and the phases of the moon. Exceptional in every respect, this historical design combines the functions of a minute repeater, a pillar-wheel chronograph, a perpetual calendar and a moonphase indicator whose 18K gold moon stands out against a lapis lazuli sky. Tradition dictated that a masterpiece of such a scale be encased in solid gold. This pocket-watch is so exclusive that only three of these intricate marvels will ever exist.

187

Vacheron Constantin

From left to right and center

THE "JALOUSIE"

The special edition "Jalousie" is strictly limited to 125 pieces. This classic, designed for men, can be found in Vacheron Constantin's "Les Historiques" Collection. Its originality lies in a unique system of 18K white gold engraved shutters which cover the dial and can be opened and closed with a small slide piece set with a sapphire cabochon. Its rectangular waterproof case is in 18K pink gold with engraved roman numerals on the bezel. They are each fitted with a hand-wound mechanical movement with a subdial for the seconds at 6 o'clock. In keeping with its strong character, these highly unusual timepieces come with a white dial with blue steel hands and gold hour markers.

"FIORENZA" WATCH FROM "LES ABSOLUES" LINE.

The square-shaped case and link-type bracelet in 18K yellow gold is enhanced with 78 diamonds totaling 2.01 carats. The dial is pavéd with 110 diamonds weighing .41 carats.

"FIORENZA" WATCH FROM "LES ABSOLUES" LINE.

In a round case version and "rivière" style bracelet in 18K yellow gold set with 154 diamonds and two pentagon-cut rubies totaling 4.87 carats. Pavéd dial with 100 diamonds weighing .37 carats.

This year, Vacheron Constantin dedicates the "Fiorenza" collection to the beauty of Woman, her sensibility and discerning elegance. With flawless diamonds, glowing, deep-hued rubies and sapphires set in lustrous white or yellow gold, the "Fiorenza" collection salutes Woman and Liberty together, as lovingly painted in Florence five centuries ago.

Vacheron Constantin's renowned "Phidias" collection is named after the famous sculptor of Ancient Greece. The woman's wristwatch made of 18K yellow gold and diamonds is the crowning glory of the line. It has a precious metal bracelet and round case, and self-winding movement with a solid platinum rotor.

Designed for today's professionally and socially active men and women, "Phidias" timepieces display clean fluid lines stressed by fine detailing and finish. A variety of functions and features are available, including royal chronometers, chronographs, and GMTs. "Les Historiques" timepieces offer a variety of attractive styles and shapes reflecting the tastes of the age: cases come in a choice of silhouettes with unexpected details. "Les Historiques" also salute Geneva's distinguished craft tradition with watches with fine enamel painted cases.

Ultimate watchmakers, the artisans of Vacheron Constantin, perpetuate hand-crafted masterworks of art and

From left to right , top to bottom

MEN'S "PHIDIAS" WATCH

This 18K yellow gold model features a silvered, engine-turned dial with 18K yellow gold markers protected by a sapphire crystal on a 18K yellow gold bracelet with folding clasp. Fitted with a self-winding mechanical movement, it features a small date calendar at 3 o'clock and sweep second. The Royal Chronometers are officially certified by the COSC, "Contrôle Officiel Suisse des Chronomètres."

WOMEN'S "PHIDIAS" WATCH

Named after the famous sculptor of Ancient Greece, this 18K yellow gold automatic watch features a diamond bezel and a silvered, engine-turned dial enhanced with 11 diamond markers and protected by a sapphire crystal on an 18K gold bracelet with folding clasp. Water resistant to 5 atm.

WOMEN'S "TONNEAU" FROM "LES ESSENTIELLES."

This 18K yellow gold barrel-shaped watch displays a silvered engine turned dial with four Arabic and eight stud markers and a gold basket-weave bracelet. Water resistant to 30m, it features a hand-wound mechanical movement.

THE "SOVEREIGN"

Matching 18K rose gold "Sovereign" watches for men and women from Vacheron Constantin's "Les Essentielles" model line. Both feature a round diamond set case, white dials with 12 diamond hour markers and an attractive, highly original bracelet. Hand-wound mechanical movement.

engineering, with the same dedication for refinement and innovation it has enjoyed since its creation. Today, leaders of the company follow in the footsteps of the founders. "The watchmakers of Vacheron Constantin today are re-creating a classic legacy as they introduce new designs that retain from the past what the present can not improve." Vacheron Constantin will always do better with the impossible...

189

From left to right

"TONNEAU"

Matching 18K white gold diamond set "Tonneau." The barrel-shaped watches for him and her both feature a diamond bezel, silvered engine turned dial with 12 diamond hour markers and woven bracelet partially pavéd with diamonds. With hand-wound mechanical movement and sapphire crystal.

"KALLA PAGODE"

From "Les Absolues" line. Both its rectangular case and its bracelet are in 18K white gold and entirely set with 264 baguette-cut diamonds weighing some 60 carats. Meticulously selected and matched with respect to cut, color and clarity, then painstakingly set by the experienced master jeweler. The dial itself is "cobbled" with an additional 48 baguette-cut stones totaling about 5 carats. The crystal is made of corundum, the hardest natural substance after the diamond. Individually numbered, the watch comes with a certificate of authenticity.

Bibliography

The Art of Breguet: An Important Collection of
204 Watches, Clocks and Wristwatches.
(Geneva: Habsburg Fine Art Auctioneers
Antiquorum, 1991).

I.W.C. - International Watch Co., Schaffhausen.
Hans-F. Tolke & Jurgen King.
(Zurich: Verlag Ineichen, 1987).

The Grande Complication by I.W.C.
Manfred Fritz.
(Schaffhausen: Edition Stemmle, 1991).

*Watches: Porsche Design by I.W.C.
(Schaffhausen: International Watch Co. AG, 1993)

*Watches from I.W.C.
(Schaffhausen: International Watch Co. AG, 1993)

Reverso - The Living Legend.
Manfred Fritz.
(Edition Braus, 1992).

*Timepieces from the "Manufacture."
(Jaeger-LeCoultre, 1993-4).

Patek Philippe, Genève.
Martin Huber & Alan Banbery.
(Zurich: Verlag Peter Ineichen, 1982).

Patek Philippe, Genève, Antiquorum.
Martin Huber & Alan Banbery
(Geneva: Patek Philippe S.A., 1988).

Patek Philippe, Genève.
Martin Huber & Alan Banbery.
(Geneva: Patek Philippe S.A., 1993).

Universal Genève: 100 Ans de Tradition
Horlogère.
Italo Bonifacio & Laura Rivolta.
(Rome: Editions Sothis Éditrice, 1995)

Masterpieces of Classical Watchmaking.
G.L.Brunner, C.Pfeiffer-Belli, & M.K.Wehrli.
(Munchen, Audemars Piguet, Le Brassus/CH, 1993)

Le Collezioni Orologi: Meccanici Piu' Prestigiosi
del Mondo. Maurizio Zinelli, dir.
(Rome: Editoriale Tourbillon S.r.l., 1995)

Dictionnaire Professionnel Illustré de
L'Horlogerie. G.-A. Berner.
(Bienne: La Société du Journal La Suisse
Horlogère S.A., 1988).

Dictionnaire Technologique des Parties
de la Montre, 2ème édition.
(Neuchâtel: Ebauches S.A., 1953).

Handbook of Watch and Clock Repairs.
H.G. Harris.
(New York: Emerson Books, Inc., 1969).

Histoire et Technique de La Montre Suisse.
Eugène Jaquet & Alfred Chapuis.
(Editions Urs Graf Bale et Olten, 1945).

The Joseph Bulova School of Watchmaking
Training Manual, 12ème édition.
(New York: Joseph Bulova School of
Watchmaking, 1980).

Masterpieces of Watchmaking, Vol.I.
Luigi Pippa.
(Milano: Sperling & Kupfer Editori S.p.A., 1966)

La Montre: Principes et Méthodes de
Fabrication. George Daniels.
(Editions Scriptar S.A., 1993).

Montres et horlogers exceptionnels de la Vallée
de Joux.
Daniel Aubert.
(Neuchâtel: Editions Antoine Simonin, 1993).

L'Orologio Conoscerlo per Amarlo.
Italo Bonifacio.
(Rome: Sothis Editrice Srl, 1993).

La Saga des Cartier.
Gilberte Gautier.
(Paris: Editions Michel Lafont, 1988).

The World of Vacheron Constantin, Genève.
Carole Lambelet & Lorette Coen.
(Geneva: Editions Scriptar SA/Vacheron
Constantin Genève. S.A. , 1992).

Wristwatches: A Handbook & Price Guide.
Gisbert Brunner & Christian Pfeiffer-Belli.
(Atglen: Schiffer Publishing Ltd., 1993).

Wristwatches: History of a Century's
Development. Kahlert, Muhe, & Brunner.
(Atglen: Schiffer Publishing Ltd., 1986).